GW00673820

The Purpose of God

The Purpose of God

An exposition of Ephesians

R C Sproul

Christian Focus Publications

© R C Sproul
ISBN 1-85792-609-9

Published in 1994 as part of the Focus on the Bible Commentary series.
Reprinted in 2002 and 2006
by
Christian Focus Publications, Geanies House,
Fearn, Ross-shire, IV20 1TW, Scotland.

www.christianfocus.com

Cover design by Alister MacInnes

Printed and bound by
WS Bookwell, Finland

Scripture quotations, unless otherwise indicated, are from
The New International Version

Contents

Introduction
(1:1-2)

Paul, an apostle of Christ Jesus by the will of God,
    To the saints in Ephesus, the faithful in Christ Jesus:
    Grace and peace to you from God our Father and the
Lord Jesus Christ.

Where was the letter sent?

The New International Version has the words **to the saints in Ephesus** but many other modern translations delete the words *in Ephesus* from the translation of the text, and simply announce that this is a letter from Paul. Why the discrepancy?

There is a tremendously fascinating mystery about whether or not this book was ever intended for the Ephesians in particular. For centuries no-one challenged the widely-held belief and tradition that originally Paul wrote this letter to the church in Ephesus in Asia Minor. But recent scholarship has raised various questions about its destination. Serious questions have also arisen in recent years as to who wrote the epistle. Did it really come from the hand of the apostle Paul or was it written by someone else? Before we plunge into the content of this book we need to consider some of these preliminary questions.

The fact that a majority of versions contain the words, 'in Ephesus', and other versions don't, is not because Bible translators are being hyper-critical or arbitrary. The problem boils down to a question of *textual criticism*. A person doesn't have to be a Greek scholar or a professional theologian to take some interest in this science. Textual criticism is the attempt to reconstruct, as accurately as possible, the original Greek text of the New Testament.

When this letter was written in the first century, it was written in the Greek language. Then it went to its destination, where it was read and preserved before being copied for the next generation. Those copies were then copied, and soon copies were spread all over the world, wherever Christians were to be found. The original letter that was penned by the apostle has long since been lost but various copies have survived down to this day.

Scholars in textual criticism examine very carefully all the surviving copies of the New Testament literature. And it has been said, of the manuscripts that survive that they agree 99% with each other because the copying process in the Ancient World was carried out very carefully and meticulously. We do, however, find some discrepancies in the copies. So there are copies of this letter which have the words 'in Ephesus', and other copies that omit those words.

The majority of surviving manuscripts contain the words 'in Ephesus'. That is the reason why, for centuries, the church kept this particular designation and variant in the English version of the New Testament. There are only two or three significant copies that do not have these words. The unfortunate problem is, however, that two of the very finest and most trustworthy of the surviving manuscripts from the ancient world are the very copies that don't have the words 'in Ephesus'. For this reason, the evidence is almost equally weighted for and against the inclusion in the text of the term 'in Ephesus'. So it is possible that the designated destination was never part of the original epistle.

There are other factors that biblical commentators consider have a bearing on this decision. We know from Luke's record in the Acts of the Apostles that, during his third missionary journey, Paul stayed in Ephesus for two years. A congregation developed there in which he obviously had a very important and vital ministry. Normally, whenever Paul writes back to churches where he knows individuals personally, he gives personal greetings to his dear brothers and sisters who are still alive in those congregations. That kind of personal communication is glaringly absent from the letter to the Ephesians. This does not necessarily prohibit the possibility that the original destination was the Ephesian congregation, but it provides added support for the idea that perhaps this letter was not originally destined specifically for the congregation at Ephesus.[1]

The majority viewpoint today is that, in all probability, the epistle to the Ephesians was written originally as a circular letter. Rather than the apostle writing a specific message to a particular congregation concerning a definite problem that had arisen, Paul wrote an epistle that he intended would be circulated to all of the churches in Asia Minor. This explains why Paul refrains from his normal, specified greetings to particular individuals. It seems likely that Paul, towards the end of his life, had a burden to write to the church in general, a synopsis of the revelation that was given to him as the apostle of Jesus Christ, a summary of the great truths of Christianity. What follows is written on the assumption that this letter was originally written by the apostle to be circulated to a large number of churches in Asia Minor.

Ephesus in the first century

The book of Revelation contains messages to seven cities of Asia Minor. Asia Minor was, in Paul's day, the Roman province of Proconsular Asia. The book of Revelation speaks of Ephesus, Smyrna, Pergamum, Thyatira, Sardis, Philadelphia, and Laodicea.

These seven cities were arranged around the urban hub of

---

1. Having been linked with the International Council on Biblical Inerrancy, I believe the Bible to be the Word of God, inspired by the Holy Spirit. We need, however, to distinguish textual criticism (which I call lower criticism) from what is often referred to as Higher Criticism (higher critical scholars carry no brief for the inspiration of the Scriptures and say that in the original there were errors and mistakes). Lower criticism is called 'lower' because it doesn't involve any academic criticism of the content of Scripture itself. Its analysis is simply focused on the question of trying to reconstruct the original manuscripts. The reason why textual criticism has been such a fascinating and rigorous scientific process is because the church has confessed her belief that the original manuscripts were written under divine inspiration. But classical Protestantism, for the most part, has been very careful to say that our belief in the infallibility and inspiration of Scripture is not a belief in the inspiration of translations. We recognise that translations differ from each other, and sometimes even contradict each other. Conservative Christianity has been very jealous to say that inspiration belongs only to the original autographs of Scripture.

the province, with Ephesus occupying a strategic point. If Ephesians was a letter intended for all the churches in the area, it may have followed a circular route round these cities.

Ephesus itself was the gateway to Asia. It was at the mouth of the important Cayster River and functioned in a way similar to colonial Pittsburgh (Fort Pitt). Pittsburgh was called the 'Gateway to the West' because of the formation of the Ohio River that flows west to the Mississippi. Waterways were crucial links of transportation and commerce before the advent of mechanized travel. A highway to Ephesus also served as a hub for caravan travel (much as Chicago did for rail transportation). In ancient history the Greeks and the Romans both vied for control of Ephesus because of its strategic military and commercial location.

Ephesus was famous for its great temple, a shrine to the goddess Diana (or Artemis in Greek). The temple of Diana was one of the seven wonders of the world. It was 425 feet in length and 220 feet in breadth. Architecturally it was composed of 127 white marble columns, each 62 feet high. It was opulently decorated with ornate carvings and priceless paintings. Its chief attraction, however, was an image of Diana said to have fallen directly from heaven to earth. The temple was so popular among pagans that Ephesus emerged as the religious centre of all Asia.

A stadium was built near the temple during the reign of Nero (AD 54–68), coinciding with Paul's visit between 53–56. The stadium had a seating capacity of about 25,000, at a time when Ephesus had a population of about 250,000 people. This stadium was the scene of the riot against Paul and his friends.

The temple of Diana had close links to local commerce and it was also a tourist centre. The temple cult involved worship of Diana as fertility goddess and as goddess of the woods and hunt. Diana's image represented the figure of a crowned woman with multiple breasts to signify fertility. In addition to the Diana cult, Ephesus was also known as a centre of occult arts and practices.

The account of Paul's sojourn in Ephesus (Acts 19) indicates that the apostle had conflicts with various branches of the pagan community. These conflicts were a direct result of Paul's powerful ministry in the area:

> **Paul entered the synagogue and spoke boldly there for three months, arguing persuasively about the kingdom of God. But some of them became obstinate; they refused to believe and publicly maligned the Way. So Paul left them. He took the disciples with him and had discussions daily in the lecture hall of Tyrannus. This went on for two years, so that all the Jews and Greeks who lived in the province of Asia heard the word of the Lord** (Acts 19:8-10).

In the Acts of the Apostles, Luke reports that God worked extraordinary miracles by Paul, so that even **handkerchiefs and aprons that had touched him were taken to the sick, and their illnesses were cured and the evil spirits left them** (19:12).

Paul's impact on the practitioners of the occult resulted in a massive book-burning: **A number who had practised sorcery brought their scrolls together and burned them publicly. When they calculated the value of the scrolls, the total came to fifty thousand drachmas** (Acts 19:19).

Luke's comment about of the value of the books that were burned indicates the commercial crisis that was involved in Paul's influence against paganism. The current value of the fifty thousand drachmas is close to $500,000.

The reaction of those with a vested commercial interest in the pagan practices was swift:

> **About that time there arose a great disturbance about the Way. A silversmith named Demetrius, who made silver**

shrines of Artemis, brought in no little business for the craftsmen. He called them together, along with the workmen in related trades, and said: "Men, you know we receive a good income from this business. And you see and hear how this fellow Paul has convinced and led astray large numbers of people here in Ephesus and in practically the whole province of Asia. He says that man-made gods are no gods at all. There is danger not only that our trade will lose its good name, but also that the temple of the great goddess Artemis will be discredited, and the goddess herself, who is worshipped throughout the province of Asia and the world, will be robbed of her divine majesty."

When they heard this, they were furious and began shouting: "Great is Artemis of the Ephesians!" (Acts 19:23-28).

The riot at Ephesus was triggered by Paul's teaching that 'man-made gods are no gods at all'. Christianity makes no peace with idolatry. The scene at Ephesus was that of the triumph of the gospel over pagan idolatry.

The temple of Diana was once one of the seven wonders of the world. Today it has no members. Diana was not so great after all.

Was Paul the author?

The first verse identifies the author as Paul, the apostle. It reads, **Paul, an apostle of Christ Jesus by the will of God. To the saints in Ephesus, the faithful in Christ Jesus.** There are no variant manuscript readings that would suggest a textual problem here in copying or transmission of the original; all the texts agree that Paul was its author. This fact went unchallenged for virtually 1800 years of church history. Only with the advent of modern forms of criticism has his authorship been questioned. There are now many in the critical world who have become convinced that Paul did not, in fact, write this letter to the Ephesians.

The reasons that are set forth to argue against Paul's authorship of Ephesians include the following considerations. First, there is an unusually large number of instances of what are called *hupurx legomena*, a technical term that refers to words which occur only once in the body of a person's total literary output. In other words, if we catalogue all the letters that we know were written by Paul, construct a vocabulary list of his language, and count up the number of times he uses each word, we discover that there were certain words which occur only once in all his writings. In Ephesians we have almost fifty of these words. If Paul did write it, how can we account for this?

We can begin by noting that the style of the letter is affected by the fact that it is a 'circular'. Such letters are more formal than personal ones. Further the tone of Ephesians is so contemplative at points, that it sounds more like a prayer than a letter, more like a doxology than a sermon. Such a style demands its own vocabulary.

Is it not arrogant to assume that the apostle Paul's knowledge, linguistic skills and vocabulary were so limited that he did not have the capacity to write a letter in which he uses forty-nine words that he does not use elsewhere? Frankly, I give virtually no credence to the whole issue of *haparx legomena* as a method of determining authorship.

A second consideration brought forth is that Paul makes no mention of any personal friends or co-labourers in the Ephesian letter. Since Paul had been the founder of the Ephesian congregation, it seems rather strange that he doesn't make any direct mention of these people. This argument falls, however, if this letter was intended to be a circular epistle to a large number of churches.

A third argument set forth against Paul's authorship is this: the author of Ephesians speaks of the prophets and the apostles as being the *foundation* of the church (2:20). Critics say that this is inconsistent with the teaching of Paul found elsewhere in his epistles, where he says that the only foundation that can be laid for the church is Christ Jesus. It is unthinkable, so the argument goes, that a genuine apostle would pre-empt the glory and pre-eminence of Jesus by inserting himself and his cohorts in that primary position of being the foundation of the church.

In response, it can be argued that, rather than being contradictory, these pictures are completely harmonious. In describing the church as a building, Paul speaks of Jesus as the cornerstone. Now the cornerstone is that which holds the foundation together. In the metaphor, Jesus is not the complete foundation, but he is the chief building block, the chief cornerstone, that holds it all together.

Also, what Paul says about the apostles being the foundation is not inconsistent with what other authors of the New Testament wrote. For example, in the book of Revelation, in the vision that is unfolded of the New Jerusalem, we are told that the foundation of the heavenly city is the apostles (21:14). Therefore the metaphor of the apostolic group being the foundation of the church is consistent with the overall teaching of the New Testament. So far from it indicating that Paul is trying to usurp or supplant the authority of Christ, he is simply communicating what Jesus himself taught in the Gospels, that he would build his church upon the apostles.

Paul is very concerned, not only in this epistle but consistently through his writings, to call attention to the significance of the apostolic office. It was necessary for his readers to understand that an apostle was not one who spoke, or wrote, or taught, his own opinions. That is why, in the first verse of Ephesians, Paul says he was **an apostle of Christ Jesus, by the will of God**. The word that is translated *the will* is a form of the word *theleme* (*thelemetos*), which is a strong word indicating Divine sovereignty. Paul is declaring that he is an apostle, not by self-appointment, but through the authoritative decree, the sovereign will of Almighty God.

There is every reason to affirm what the epistle claims, namely, that it was written by the apostle Paul to the churches in Asia Minor.

1
Paul's Praise of the Father
(1:3-14)

Praise be to the God and Father of our Lord Jesus Christ, who has blessed us in the heavenly realms with every spiritual blessing in Christ. For he chose us in him before the creation of the world to be holy and blameless in his sight. In love he predestined us to be adopted as his sons through Jesus Christ, in accordance with his pleasure and will — to the praise of his glorious grace, which he has freely given us in the One he loves. In him we have redemption through his blood, the forgiveness of sins, in accordance with the riches of God's grace that he lavished on us with all wisdom and understanding. And he made known to us the mystery of his will according to his good pleasure, which he purposed in Christ, to be put into effect when the times will have reached their fulfilment — to bring all things in heaven and on earth together under one head, even Christ.

In him we were also chosen, having been predestined according to the plan of him who works out everything in conformity with the purpose of his will, in order that we, who were the first to hope in Christ, might be for the praise of his glory. And you also were included in Christ when you heard the word of truth, the gospel of your salvation. Having believed, you were marked in him with a seal, the promised Holy Spirit, who is a deposit guaranteeing our inheritance until the redemption of those who are God's possession — to the praise of his glory.

Blessing and communion

Praise be to the God and Father of our Lord Jesus Christ, who has blessed us in the heavenly realms with every spiritual blessing in Christ. Paul begins this epistle with a benediction, a doxology, a hymn of praise and thanksgiving to God. It flows out of an apostolic heart that is expressing a profound sense of gratitude and acknowledged dependence upon the grace of God. Actually, in the Greek text, the word that is rendered *praise* can also be translated *blessing*. Literally, the apostle is saying: 'Blessed be the God the Father of our Lord Jesus Christ, who in turn has blessed us in the heavenly realms with every spiritual blessing in Christ.' Paul is praising or blessing God in response to the fact that God has blessed his people. The reason why different translations make use of the word *praise* is because Paul cannot bless God in the same way as God blesses him. When God blesses believers, he bestows a certain favour upon them that they do not deserve. When they bless him, it is an act of praise and adoration that he richly deserves. It is not an act of grace on their part to give benediction or blessing to the Almighty.

Commentators struggle with understanding what Paul means with *blessed us in the heavenly realms in Christ*. I believe that Paul does not only mean that the blessings received through Christ are spiritual and proceed to believers from the heavenly realms. Rather, he incorporates them as participants in some way in the heavenly realms, because they are blessed in these heavenly places *with* Christ. One commentator suggests that Paul is reflecting on his own mystical experience in the third heaven, where he was enraptured by an overwhelming sense of being close to the presence of Jesus.

There is, however, a mystical communion that the believers

enjoy with Christ through the Holy Spirit. It is not an out-of-body experience, or transportation of the soul into the heavenly regions, or astral projection. Nevertheless, there is a real communion, a certain sense of Christ being made present to us by the Holy Spirit. As has often been said, 'Touching his human nature, Jesus is no longer present with us. Touching his Divine nature, he is never absent from us.' Jesus, in the Gospels, refers to leaving, departing from his disciples and returning to heaven (John 7:33; 14:1-4), and yet at the same time says, 'I am with you always ...' (Matthew 28:20).

We usually understand Christians' enjoyment of the presence of Christ as referring to the Spirit bringing Christ to his people, by bridging the gap between heaven and earth. But in this passage there is the suggestion that it refers not to the Spirit present with us, but us present to the risen Christ. Mystically, we move from earth to heaven, because we have fellowship with Christ in the heavenly realms.

Election and predestination

Paul moves immediately, without any apology, to a bold declaration of election, a doctrine which causes more consternation than any other among Christian people. But Paul doesn't hesitate:

> **For he chose us in him before the creation of the world to be holy and blameless in his sight. In love he predestined us to be adopted as his sons through Jesus Christ, in accordance with his pleasure and will – to the praise of his glorious grace, which he has freely given us in the One he loves.**

First of all, we are to remember that the apostle does not use the terms *election* and *predestination* in some vague, philosophical sense of grim determinism. We must understand these concepts in two very important broader contexts.

The first is that election and predestination belong to the

whole scope of salvation. That may be obvious, but so often when we struggle with the doctrine of predestination and election it is because our eyes are always fixed on the difficulty of resolving predestination with human freedom. The Bible, however, links them with salvation, which every Christian should find enormously comforting. Salvation is not an afterthought of God. The redemption of his people, the salvation of his church, my eternal salvation, these actions are not a postscript to the Divine activity. Instead, from the very foundation of the world, God had a sovereign plan to save a significant portion of the human race, and he moves heaven and earth to bring it to pass.

Secondly, this matter of individuals being chosen before the foundation of the world by the predestinating love of God is always understood to be *in Christ*. It is with a view to Christ that believers were incorporated in the Divine plan of salvation.

An alternative explanation of election has always troubled me. Some describe it in this way: God looks down the tunnel of time from all eternity, observing human responses, and so he knows what choices will be made when people are invited to respond to the gospel of Christ. On the basis of that foreknowledge and on the basis of these foreseen choices of human beings, God then elects people to be saved. So our salvation, our election, is *conditional* upon the foreseen choices that we make.

But if salvation ultimately rests upon the foreseen responses of fallen human beings to the invitation of the gospel, we might well despair of anyone ever being saved. People who are dead in sin, who are by nature at enmity with God, who walk in the ways of the prince of the power of the air, would never make a positive response to the gospel. Consequently, the only one who would occupy heaven would be Christ the Redeemer himself. Christ would be a Saviour without having saved anyone. That is, if this view of man's ability to choose

God unaided, or choose Christ without the predestinating grace of the Father to make that certain, is the case.

But what we see here is that our election is *in Christ*. Christ is the Beloved and we are chosen by the Father *in* the Beloved, and *for* the Beloved. Remember Jesus' prayer in the upper room, when he thanks the Father for those whom the Father has given him, and his exclamation of confidence that all that the Father has given to him will come to him (John 17).

God chose his people in Christ, before the creation of the world, *to be holy and blameless in his sight*: that is, he set them apart to be a consecrated people, known as saints. Again, the goal of predestination is *adoption*. It was God's good pleasure not only to prepare the kingdom for his Son, but also for those whom he adopted in his Son, the heirs of God and joint-heirs with Christ. Election is in Christ, leading to adoption into the family of God.

Paul says that God has done this in *accordance with his pleasure and will*. This is the only reason to be found in Scripture that explains why God elects people for salvation. The reason for election is not my foreseen righteousness; or my foreseen obedience; or my foreseen response to the gospel.

Somebody will say that this smacks of an arbitrary, capricious God who plays a game of salvation-roulette and takes delight in choosing some and damning others. But we miss the point if we think in that way. Yes, salvation does relate to the pleasure of God's will, which means that God *is pleased* by exercising his will to salvation. But an arbitrary, capricious will is not a good will, it is an immoral will. There is a reason why the elect have been chosen to salvation, but the reason is to be found in God and not in them. In other words, God did not choose them because they qualified for the choice. Rather, he chose them because he was pleased to extend mercy to them, while the others he passes over. God is not obligated to save anybody, to make any special act of grace, to draw anyone to himself. He could leave the whole world to perish, and such would be a righteous judgment.

Where we struggle with predestination is at this point: that God leaves some to themselves, but in other cases he intervenes. He gives a blessing to his elect that he does not give to other people. This means that God does not treat everybody alike. Indeed, Scripture from beginning to end makes it abundantly clear that God doesn't treat everybody the same. He appeared to Abraham, called him out of godless paganism and made him the father of a great nation, but he did not do that for Pharaoh. Jesus appeared to the enemy of the church, Paul, on the road to Damascus and overcame his unbelief right there, but he did not do that for Pontius Pilate or for Caiaphas. Would it not be a ghastly thing to suggest that the reason why Jesus revealed himself to Paul and not to Pilate, was because Paul in some manner deserved or earned or merited that special revelation?

Think of it in this very personal way. If you are a believer, ask yourself candidly why it is that you believe yet somebody else does not. Do you harbour the idea within your heart that the reason why you received Christ while your neighbour rejected him is because you were somehow more righteously disposed towards obeying the summons of the gospel than your neighbour?

Why doesn't God give his grace to everyone? It is certainly a legitimate question, but we do not know the answer. We might suggest that God is honoured when his justice is manifested in leaving some to the punishment their sins deserve, and he is honoured when his grace is manifested in the salvation of his elect. Of course, God is also just when he gives grace, for election is inseparably bound up with Christ. It is for the sake of the Beloved, and not just because of God's love for us, that there is redemption at all. God honours his Beloved Son by creating from fallen humanity new vessels of life, a new humanity, a new household of faith, that he calls his church, those who are called out from this world, according to the sovereign plan of Divine election.

Redemption

Once I was speaking in Philadelphia and, after my address, there was an open question and answer session. I had been talking about the problem of guilt that plagues people in this world. One woman responded during the discussion and somewhat agitatedly said: 'Why do you have to speak about guilt? It seems to me that you are taking a rather downbeat view of Christianity.' All this preoccupation with sin and atonement did not interest her. She wanted to speak about Christianity in a more positive light, what it has to say about brotherly love, concern for our fellow man and the love and kindness of God. She obviously was recoiling from this focus upon sin and guilt. I tried to explain that if we are going to be honest in our reading of the Scriptures then we don't have the option of picking and choosing those elements of the Biblical message that we find particularly suitable to our environment. First of all, before any application of the Scriptures can be made, we must understand the basic thrust of the message.

We are living in a time when there has been a wholesale attempt to reconstruct Christianity apart from its central focus on personal salvation. That is to say, it seems as if people today want a Christianity without redemption. But we cannot avoid the fact that at the heart of the teaching of Jesus and of the apostolic message is a God who redeems his people.

Ephesians begins with the vast, cosmic purview of Divine activity. The majestic viewpoint of this chapter stands in stark contrast to the worldly character of the spirit of our own age. Paul reminds his readers that the whole scope of reality is under the sovereign control and authority of God. The ultimate concern and plan of God is redemption. Redemption is not a peripheral matter, rather it cuts to the very core of Divine activity. From the foundation of the world God has determined to bring about redemption in Christ. **In him** (in Christ) **we have redemption through his blood, the forgiveness of sins** (verse 7).

What does *redemption* mean? Its primary usage in the Bible is to *buy back from slavery*. In the agricultural marketplace there were those who were sold as slaves. To *redeem* such persons meant to pay the purchase-price in order to release them from their bondage.

God brings about this redemption through the *blood of Christ* and this is linked, by Paul, with *the forgiveness of sins*. In the New Testament, the redemption of man is redemption from the bondage and the power of sin, involving a resolution of the power of guilt.

I labour this point because the contemporary view is that God doesn't really take sin seriously. Yes, he acknowledges that evil is evil, but what he does with evil is that he simply forgives it. The means of redemption, however, is the blood of Christ. Nothing could speak louder about how seriously God views the problem of the alienation that exists between us and him because of our rebellion through our sin. An atonement was made, a blood sacrifice was offered, and that becomes the basis of the forgiveness of sin. So redemption is accomplished through the atonement of Christ.

Redemption and the forgiveness of sins are **in accordance with the riches of God's grace that he lavished on us with all wisdom and understanding** (verses 7b- 8). This *wisdom and understanding* does not refer to our wisdom and understanding, but to God's Divine understanding, that is, the scheme of redemption he has decreed.

Paul continues: **And he made known to us the mystery of his will according to his good pleasure, which he purposed in Christ, to be put into effect when the times will have reached their fulfilment – to bring all things in heaven and on earth together under one head, even Christ** (verses 9, 10). When Paul uses the term *mystery*, our antennae should go up immediately, because in the ancient world there were various forms of religions that were called 'mystery religions'. To be a member of one of these particular groups, one had to undergo some exotic initiation rites involving, usually, a kind of occult practice. Secretly, the mysteries of the religion were revealed to them, and these were carefully guarded from the outside. But that is not what *mystery* means in the New Testament. Paul is showing that the revelation God gives of himself and of the plan of redemption is a gradual, progressive unveiling of his full and final purposes.

Think how redemption was revealed to the saints in the Old Testament. They went through elaborate rituals involving the sacrifice of animals and days of atonement. Even when God gave his promise of redemption to Abraham, he didn't spell out that there was going to be an atonement by a Saviour, through an incarnation and suffering. All he told Abraham was that, through Abraham's seed, all the nations of the world would be blessed. God didn't reveal to Abraham everything he had in mind. The details remained hidden, shrouded in mystery. Throughout the Old Testament, however, more and more of the Divine plan was being revealed. Special revelation reached its zenith with the appearance of the Son of God on earth. Through the teaching of Christ and his apostles, a quantum leap is made in terms of the content of supernatural revelation.

On another occasion when Paul refers to *mystery*, he is

referring to the inclusion of the Gentiles in the New Testament church. That had been hidden, or was vague at best, in the Old Testament. There were isolated references here and there that God's plan of salvation in the Old Testament was not limited to the Jews, but it certainly wasn't clear to what extent salvation would be extended to the Gentile world.

The goal of history

Here in Ephesians, Paul is stressing that the mystery God has made known to believers is not an abiding riddle. Rather what once was hidden is now made manifest. God **made known to us the mystery of his will according to his good pleasure, which he purposed in Christ**. In other words, God has disclosed to the church his eternal purpose and plan for what we call 'history', for space and time.

That purpose will be **put into effect when the times will have reached their fulfilment -- to bring all things in heaven and earth together under one head, even Christ**. Paul uses a concept that is integral to the New Testament teaching, seen in his use of the Greek word *pleroma* (fullness). We remember that the birth of Jesus occurred in the fullness of time, at the exact time that God had purposed. When Paul speaks of *when the times will have reached their fulfilment*, he is looking to the final *pleroma*. God has revealed to the church, through Christ, the ultimate goal of creation.

Paul's doctrine of predestination is not only concerned with individuals, but includes the destiny of world history. The destiny of creation is not an open-ended matter of chance, for God has determined from the foundation of the world how the universe is going to end up. It is not simply that he has a goal or a plan, but that he has a Divine, omnipotent ability to work out that plan. God has determined a destiny for this world.

I can't think of anything designed to create more optimism in the church of Jesus Christ, than to know that the future of this planet, the future of reality, is in the hands of God alone.

Recently I have been re-reading Leon Uris's early novel, *Exodus*, in which he traces the struggle of the modern Jew to return to the land of Israel. A movement grew spontaneously around the world, with the dream of returning to Zion. The spirit of Zionism began to grow and received tremendous impetus at the end of World War I by the ratification of the Balfour Declaration whereby fifty nations agreed to establish the modern state of Israel. But what filled the Jewish people with hope at the end of the second decade of the twentieth century was destined to be delayed for a long time.

There is a similarity between the Christian hope and the hope of the modern Jew, who looked ahead, saying, 'Next year, in Jerusalem'. Our future hope is in the consummation of the kingdom of God. Even though we live in a period that some have described as the post-Christian era, we know that God has **purposed to bring all things in heaven and on earth together under one head, even Christ**. God predestined from all eternity not only that Jesus should be Saviour, but that Jesus should be King of kings and Lord of lords. God has already crowned his Son, for the coronation has taken place in the ascension; but we live in a world that does not recognise its ruler, that does not kneel in obeisance before its appointed king. The same one through whom all things were made, by whom all things were made and for whom all things were made, will receive all things at the end of time. God's appointed plan for the universe is to bring all things on heaven and on earth together, under one head. The goal of creation is neither chaos nor disharmony but unity, and the point of unity will be his anointed king.

How does that relate to us? Well it is *in him*. Paul writes: **In him we were also chosen, having been predestined**

according to the plan of him who works out everything in conformity with the purpose of his will, in order that we, who were the first to hope in Christ, might be for the praise of his glory (verses 11,12). This universe is destined for glory and Christians are predestined to participate in and witness to that glory.

The Holy Spirit – a seal and a guarantee

Paul takes this grand and eloquent theme of the cosmic scope of things and brings it right down to his readers as individuals: **And you also were included in Christ when you heard the word of truth, the gospel of your salvation** (verse 13). He says that their salvation is part of this grand destiny that God has determined for the universe.

The term *heard* is amplified in the next few words. There are many people who have heard the gospel in the sense that the sound of it has struck their auditory nerves. They have been exposed to it, but they have never submitted to it. But in the case of the Ephesians, it was combined with faith in Christ.

Paul goes on to say that *having believed*, they **were marked in him with a seal, the promised Holy Spirit, who is a deposit guaranteeing our inheritance until the redemption of those who are God's possession – to the praise of his glory** (verses 13, 14). The NIV uses the concepts *marked with a seal* and the *deposit guaranteeing our inheritance*. Banks give guarantees concerning your deposits. But there is no bank in this world that can give you an absolute guarantee for there is no bank that is incapable of going under. There is no government on this earth that can absolutely guarantee your investment or your inheritance or your deposit. As a result of having heard and believed the gospel, however, the Holy Spirit comes into our lives to seal us and to give us the guarantee of our inheritance.

The word for *sealing* is used only a very few times in the New Testament. The concept is of an indelible mark, representing a promise. The closest thing to this in the ancient world would be whenever a king wanted to authenticate a decree and marked it with a wax impression from his signet ring. This signet ring wax impression, in the Greek world, was called a *throgos*, a seal, and it represented and guaranteed that what had been promised would take place.

Christians debate whether it is possible for a Christian to lose his salvation. I believe that if we were left to ourselves then it would not only be possible for us to lose our salvation, but I wonder if it would be possible for anybody to persevere in salvation. But my perseverance in the faith does not rest in my own ability to persevere. My conviction that no Christian is ever lost is based on the promises of God and on statements like this from the first chapter of Ephesians: that when we believe in Jesus Christ, God the Holy Spirit is sealed on us and our souls are marked indelibly as the children of God.

The Authorised Version translates 'deposit' as the *earnest* of the Spirit. About the only way we use that word today, in the USA, is in real estate. Perhaps you have had the experience of looking for a home. When you finally found a house you wanted to buy, you didn't want to lose it to somebody else. So, before you went to the bank to get your loan, the agent asked for what is called 'pin money' or 'earnest money'. In exchange, he will take the house off the market while you are trying to secure your loan to purchase the house. It is an initial payment that you will forfeit if you back out of the deal. It is a sign, a concrete token, that you are serious about buying this house, that you are in earnest. The same happened in the ancient world of commerce where, when a person gave his initial promissory down-payment, the implication was that this money was a token of a promise to pay the rest.

Although believers have not seen the total redemption that God has planned for them, it is guaranteed. God has personally pledged it by marking each of them with the seal of the promised Holy Spirit.

2
Paul's First Prayer for his Readers (1:15-23)

For this reason, ever since I heard about your faith in the Lord Jesus and your love for all the saints, I have not stopped giving thanks for you, remembering you in my prayers. I keep asking that the God of our Lord Jesus Christ, the glorious Father, may give you the Spirit of wisdom and revelation, so that you may know him better. I pray also that the eyes of your heart may be enlightened in order that you may know the hope to which he has called you, the riches of his glorious inheritance in the saints, and his incomparably great power for us who believe. That power is like the working of his mighty strength, which he exerted in Christ when he raised him from the dead and seated him at his right hand in the heavenly realms, far above all rule and authority, power and dominion, and every title that can be given, not only in the present age but also in the one to come. And God placed all things under his feet and appointed him to be head over everything for the church, which is his body, the fulness of him who fills everything in every way.

Although Christianity is not mysticism, there are profoundly mystical and spiritual dimensions that are inseparably bound up with the Christian faith. The message so focuses on the work of the Holy Spirit in our lives, and on the concept of supernatural and divine revelation, that we must be careful to rid our minds of the cross secularism that threatens to extinguish the Biblical message in our day.

For this reason refers back to what Paul wrote about the salvation that God has brought to pass in Christ and the giving of the Holy Spirit into the lives of believers as an earnest and a seal on their souls. Paul the pastor has a profound and continuous sense of gratitude. What is moving him is the report that the early Christian community is not only exercising faith in Christ, but is showing that faith through love for one another. So he says, **since I heard about your faith in the Lord Jesus and your love for all the saints, I have not stopped giving thanks for you** (verses 15,16).

Throughout the ages the church has understood that the most significant manifestation of true faith is love. Faith without love is not faith, only speculation or knowledge or mere intellectual assent. The fruit of authentic faith is always love. Paul is expressing his joy and delight that this kind of love is flowing from the faith of these people.

In his prayers for them he asks **that the God of our Lord Jesus Christ, the glorious Father, may give you the Spirit of wisdom and revelation** (verse 17). Paul is speaking to believers, so we have to understand that he is not talking about the initial opening of the eyes of the Christian to the truth of the gospel. Although they have been sealed by the Spirit, they need the Spirit to be their ongoing teacher, instructing them by giving them *wisdom* and *revelation*. Those two things are inseparably related. The Old Testament teaching that the fear of the Lord is the beginning of wisdom (Psalm 111:10) means that people only have true understanding (wisdom) when they look at everything from God's perspective. Authentic wisdom begins when we understand that God is to be the object of our devotion, our adoration, and our reverence.

Those who are impenitent lack this reverential fear for God, therefore the wisdom of which Scripture speaks is beyond their reach. But we must also notice that the fear of the Lord is the *beginning* of wisdom, not the *consummation* of wisdom. Paul is praying for his readers that this wisdom may increase, through the work of the Spirit within them and through his Divine revelation to them. God's Word is the source of all wisdom and the Spirit inspired that Word. He is the one who reveals the truth of God in the first instance and then illumines our minds in order that we may grasp it properly. Paul is not saying that Christians can expect to receive new revelations from God and so become contemporary apostles. No, he is saying that the Spirit works in Christians to help them understand the revelation (the Bible) God has already given.

The goal Paul has in mind is **so that you may know him better** (verse 17). Notice, he is still speaking in the future tense. Again, conversion does not give us a comprehensive knowledge of God. The quest, the search for the knowledge of God is a lifelong enterprise for the Christian.

In verse 18 Paul writes: **I pray also that the eyes of your heart may be enlightened.** In Alan Bloom's book, *The Closing of the American Mind*, the first sentence (a statement he amplifies throughout the rest of the volume) says that it is virtually guaranteed that any freshman who enters a college or university in the United States comes already persuaded of a relativistic view of truth. Bloom argues that far from helping the freshman to grow out of this naive and untenable position, higher education tends to reinforce the error.

One of the great values of our culture is belief in an open mind. The apostles of relativism, who teach that there are no absolutes and that there is no ultimate and eternal truth, want to suggest that the way to have an open mind is to adopt their philosophy. What is so fascinating about Bloom's critique, which does not come from a Christian perspective, is his argument that relativism is the closing of the mind to truth. At this point he is saying something that the New Testament emphasises; yes, we are to have open minds, but not so open that they will accept any doctrine or any viewpoint. The goal of the Christian life is a mind open to the teaching of God. In that sense, to be open to the teaching of God is to be open to the teaching of truth.

Paul uses a strange construction here: **the eyes of your heart may be enlightened.** Usually we think of the eyes as being in our head, and we connect the head with the brain and the brain with the mind. Hence we say that we understand a particular teaching with the mind. But the apostle refers to *the eyes of the heart.* What does he mean?

He means that by nature we are closed to the things of God. He does not mean that we cannot discuss them nor have intellectual debates about them. But the *heart* in New Testament terms refers to the central disposition, inclination, bent, or proclivity of the human soul. In simple terms, the bias. Everybody has a bias and prejudices. The word 'prejudice' is usually a pejorative term, but what it literally means is to prejudge certain things, to have a standpoint, a viewpoint.

Our natural prejudgment of reality is against God. To receive the truth of God requires that our 'anti' bias be changed. The key work of the Holy Spirit in regeneration is not giving new knowledge to the brain but changing the disposition of the heart. Before the Spirit turns that heart of stone into a heart of flesh, we have no desire for the things of God. We may desire the blessings that only God can give us, but we have no affection for the things of God. At the moment of regeneration, the eyes of the heart are opened somewhat, but this is just the beginning. The whole Christian life involves an unfolding and enlarging of the heart's openness to the things of God. There are concepts, attitudes, and values in my life at present that do not please God, for there will be stony parts to my heart as long as sin abides within me. Sin clouds my thinking, my will, my desires, my affections. There will always be parts of me that need to be opened more and more to let the fullness of God's truth dwell in me.

In this latter part of the chapter, Paul mentions the triad of virtues: faith, love and hope. He is grateful for the faith that is manifesting itself in love, and now he is asking that through the wisdom of God and the opening of the soul and the heart to the knowledge of God, they will come to understand the Christian hope: **in order that you may know the hope to which he has called you, the riches of his glorious inheritance in the saints, and his incomparably great power for us who believe** (verses 18, 19). Hope is called the anchor of the soul (Hebrews 6:19), because it gives stability to the Christian life. But hope is not simply a 'wish' (I wish that such-and-such would take place); rather, it is that which latches on to the certainty of the promises of the future that God has made.

There is an attempt, in our day, to replace the emphasis in Christianity upon personal salvation and redemption with an accent on this world, this life, and a humanitarian lifestyle. Very little attention is given to a future hope. But the source of the power to live out that high ethic and to care for the people who are around us in this world, to really have compassion for man as man, is rooted and grounded in the fact that man has a future destiny that is so rich and so wonderful. By knowing the hope that is set before them, believers are motivated by the certainty that their work in this world and their care for people in the here and now, is not in vain. Paul wants their minds to be opened to know the hope to which they have been called; to know how rich are the wonderful blessings that God promises his people; to know how great is his power at work in those who believe.

That power is like the working of his mighty strength, which he exerted in Christ when he raised him from the dead and seated him at his right hand in the heavenly realms, far above all rule and authority, power and dominion, and every title that can be given, not only in the present age but also in the one to come. And God placed all things under his feet and appointed him to be head over everything for the church, which is his body, the fulness of him who fills everything in every way (verses 19-23).

How great is this power that is working within the lives of Christians? Sometimes believers feel so impotent. They see themselves as spiritual failures because the power of the flesh is so great, the temptations of this world so overwhelming, and their progress so slim. The answer to this outlook is to understand the greatness of this power. The power within us is the same as that which God used when he raised Christ from death and seated him at his right hand in the heavenly world. In other words, Paul is referring to the work of the Holy Spirit. The Holy Spirit not only raised Jesus from the dead, he raised him to the seat of cosmic authority in the universe. He raised him not only from a tomb, but from this planet to the heavenly places where he is seated on high as the exalted Lord of heaven and earth.

Paul is stressing that, at this very moment, Christ reigns in heaven as the King over all heavenly rulers, authorities, powers, and lords. The Lord Jesus is above all titles of power in this world and the next. He has authority over kings, prime ministers and presidents, over every being, every angel, good or bad, even the archangels. God put all things under Christ's feet for the church. He is now the supreme Lord over all things.

Christ has been appointed from the foundation of the world to be the head of the church. God has given to this One who is the head of all things, a body, which is the church. This is a very mystical and spiritual viewpoint.

The statement **the fulness of him who fills everything in every way** is very difficult to understand and it has occasioned tremendous discussion by New Testament scholars. To be honest with you, I don't know anybody who can say with absolute certainty what Paul means here in this verse. He uses a loaded term and even adds a pun. He uses a term, a form of *pleroma*, which refers to the fullness of things.

Some interpret Paul as saying that Christ's fullness is completed by the addition of the church to himself. As the body is given to the head, as the bridegroom receives the bride, so the church then fills up part of the plenitude of the very essence of Christ.

The other important view of this is simply to say that Christ fills the universe because he himself is the *pleroma*, the fullness of God. The fullness of God dwells in Jesus and, since Jesus permeates the whole scope of his dominions, out of that fullness, he draws to himself the church. And so in a secondary sense, the church participates in the blessing of being linked to the one in whom resides all fullness.

Either way, fullness is a loaded term with respect to spiritual reality. Elsewhere, Scripture makes it very clear that the fullness of divine things dwells in Christ (Colossians 2:9) and that the church is his mystical body (1 Corinthians 12:27; Ephesians 4:12). And the Spirit in us is the benefit which we receive by being mystically united with Jesus in whom the fullness of all things dwells.

3
The Great Change
(2:1-10)

As for you, you were dead in your transgressions and sins, in which you used to live when you followed the ways of this world and of the ruler of the kingdom of the air, the spirit who is now at work in those who are disobedient. All of us also lived among them at one time, gratifying the cravings of our sinful nature and following its desires and thoughts. Like the rest, we were by nature objects of wrath. But because of his great love for us, God, who is rich in mercy, made us alive with Christ even when we were dead in transgressions — it is by grace you have been saved. And God raised us up with Christ and seated us with him in the heavenly realms in Christ Jesus, in order that in the coming ages he might show the incomparable riches of his grace, expressed in his kindness to us in Christ Jesus. For it is by grace you have been saved, through faith — and this not from yourselves, it is the gift of God — not by works, so that no-one can boast. For we are God's workmanship, created in Christ Jesus to do good works, which God prepared in advance for us to do.

The beginning of chapter 2 is one of the most pivotal portions of the apostolic writings dealing with the question of our sinful nature. It explains human corruption in a way which, with the possible exception of segments of Romans, underscores more heavily than any other part of the New Testament our total dependence upon the grace of God and the work of the Holy Spirit in bringing us to spiritual life. In the perennial controversy between Augustinianism and various types of semi-Pelagianism, such as Arminianism, this passage is also pivotal, because the debate rages over how much moral ability natural, fallen man has left after mankind suffered spiritual death in Adam.

The question, of course, reaches its climax with the issue of whether or not a person who is unregenerate, who has not been quickened by the Holy Spirit, can, in any way, incline himself or turn himself with affection towards Christ. Classical Reformed theology is insistent that man is so fallen that he has no disposition, inclination or bent towards the things of Christ, and would never respond to the call of the gospel unless first the Holy Spirit changed the disposition of the heart through regeneration.

Fallen humanity

As for you, you were dead in your transgressions and sins, in which you used to live when you followed the ways of this world and of the ruler of the kingdom of the air, the spirit who is now at work in those who are disobedient (verses 1, 2). Paul addresses this to believers who once were in a state of spiritual death. It is important to notice that Paul uses the term *dead*, showing that the former spiritual state of these people was moribund, lifeless, and inert.

Sometimes we hear the following analogy: fallen man is so overcome by the power of sin, that he is like a person on his deathbed, who has no physical power left to save himself. If he is going to be healed he can't possibly do it through his own strength. The only way he can be made well would be if the physician gave him the medicine that is necessary to restore him. But the man is so desperately ill that he doesn't even have the power to reach out and take the medicine for himself. So the nurse approaches his bed, opens the bottle of medicine, pours it into a spoon, and then moves it over to the dying man's lips. But he must, by his own power, his own will and his own initiative, open his mouth to receive the medicine.

This analogy is often used to support a semi-Pelagian understanding of salvation. The idea is not that man is still good enough to work his way into the kingdom of God through his own merits, he can't possibly get there without grace. The grace of God is as necessary, according to semi-Pelagianism, for salvation, as medicine is to heal this dying man. But a type of co-operation must take place between the patient and the physician for the healing medicine to have its effect. What happens is that God provides the medicine and he brings it to the dying man, but the dying man must co-operate by opening his mouth to receive it.

Here we see the difference between semi-Pelagianism and Reformed theology. The Reformed view would be that man is not only critically ill, he is dead. The man doesn't even have the power to open his mouth to receive the healing medicine. Rather, the medicine has to be injected into him by the physician.

Another analogy goes like this: a man is cast into the sea who doesn't know how to swim. He is clearly about to drown; he has already gone under the water twice, and is sinking for the third time. His head is beneath the surface of the water. All that is left above the water is his outstretched hand, and the only way he can possibly be saved is if God would throw him a life-preserver. God is so accurate in throwing this life-preserver, that he throws it right up against the palm of the man's hand. But for that man to be saved, he must close his hand upon the life-preserver in order to be pulled to safety.

That again is the semi-Pelagian view which teaches that man must co-operate with this grace that God presents to him in order to be saved. The Reformed view is that the man is not going under the water for the third time, but is already drowned, spiritually. He is at the bottom of the sea, he is dead. The only way he can be saved is if God dives into the water and pulls the corpse up out of the water and brings him back to life.

With those two different views before us, let's look at what the apostle says. The image he chooses to describe fallen man's condition is the image of death: **you were dead in your transgressions and sins, in which you used to live**. Isn't that a strange conjunction? Paul is not contradicting himself. His point is to describe man's spiritual state, not his biological state. Obviously, when we come into this world we are biologically alive: we have minds that function, hearts that beat, wills that choose; we have affections, emotions, and all the rest. The problem is that even though we have the power to choose, we are dead to the things of God, and as a result have no desire for the things of God. Rather, we follow a different course. We follow it wilfully; we follow it freely, in the sense of doing what we want to do. But with respect to spiritual things, we are dead.

This is the way **in which you used to live when you followed the ways of this world and of the ruler of the kingdom of the air, the spirit who is now at work in those who are disobedient**. Augustine once said that man is like a horse, and he has one of two riders. Either the horse is ridden by Satan, or it is ridden by God. But the horse doesn't run on its own steam. Sadly, nothing is more natural to fallen man than to adopt, to embrace, and to walk according to the ways of this world in direct contrast to the way of God. The spirit who is influencing non-Christians to be disobedient is obviously a reference to Satan.

Paul is not saying that this condition was peculiar to the Ephesians, for he writes in verse 3, **All of us also lived among them at one time, gratifying the cravings of our sinful nature and following its desires and thoughts**. This is the universal condition of fallen humanity. He further elaborates upon this condition, by saying that people continually indulge their sinful desires. The apostle is not saying that fallen man lacks a will. The problem is not that man does not have the capacity to choose, his problem is that he has no desire for God. The desires of man's heart in his natural state are only wicked continuously, turned away from God.

What is meant by the concept of *total depravity* is not that man is as wicked as he could possibly be. Bad as we are, we can still conceive of ourselves doing worse things than we do. Rather, it means that sin has such a hold upon us in our natural state, that we never have a positive desire for Christ. Chapter 2 of Ephesians should always be read in close harmony with the sixth chapter of John's Gospel, where Jesus teaches that 'No-one can come to me unless the Father who sent me draws him' (John 6:44). That statement is crucial because Jesus gives a definitive statement about our helpless condition, apart from the grace of God. The word *can* describes ability. It is God who enables a person to come to Christ. Our salvation is a gift of God.

Paul continues: **Like the rest, we were by nature objects of wrath**. *Nature* does not refer to man as originally created but refers to the fallen character of man. Under the influence of humanism, people have the notion that human beings are born into this world in a state of innocence, with no bias in their hearts or wills towards either goodness or evil. It is as if every human being goes through his own probation. But of course, such an explanation begs the question: how is it, and how did it come to pass, that society is corrupt? Society is simply people, and if every individual is born innocent with no inclination towards good or evil, we would expect at least a probability factor of 50% of the people remaining innocent. We would expect to find pockets of society with hosts of sinless people. And those pockets would continue to support and engender more sinless people. But no such civilisation can be found because we are not born morally neutral; we are born fallen, we are born at enmity with God. We are born opposed to God and that is why, in our very nature, we are exposed to the wrath of God, and *justly* so.

The grace of God

I have always said that the first word in verse 4 is my favourite word in all the Bible. It is the word, *But*. As grim as this picture is of man's fallenness, Paul hastens to add: **But... God, who is rich in mercy**. God, out of the treasury of his grace, **made us alive with Christ even when we were dead in transgressions – it is by grace you have been saved**.

If you want to understand Reformed theology, read that verse a thousand times. It is the thematic passage of the gospel. The grace that brings us life comes to us at the very time we are dead in sin and trespasses. It is the act of God. Think of it in these terms. If you are a Christian, ask yourself: Why are you a Christian? Is it because you are better than others? Because you were more intelligent? If that is the reason, then certainly you have something of which to boast. But the New Testament teaches that you have nothing of

49

which to boast. You were a debtor who couldn't pay your debt and while you were dead in your sin and in your trespasses, it was God who quickened you from spiritual death. You could no more have done that yourself than Lazarus could have raised himself from the tomb. It is by grace you are saved.

Grace is defined simply as 'unmerited favour' or 'undeserved benefit'. Christians should never look at non-Christians with a spirit of contempt. Their attitude must reflect the classic saying, 'There, but for the grace of God, go I.' They have nothing of which to boast. They are redeemed not because of merit or good works, but by grace and by *grace alone*. That is the essence of Reformed theology. I believe it to be the essence of Pauline theology: we are redeemed by grace.

And God raised us up with Christ and seated us with him in the heavenly realms in Christ Jesus, in order that in the coming ages he might show the incomparable riches of his grace, expressed in his kindness to us in Christ Jesus (verses 6,7).

When Paul writes that Christ is seated, he means that Jesus is on the throne and has dominion over all things. But Paul also stresses that believers, who are united with Christ in a spiritual resurrection, have also been given dominion over the world. Of course, they do not rule in their own right, but because they are co-heirs with Christ. One way in which they are involved is through prayer when they make petitions to him concerning different areas. But it is always Christ, and not believers, who makes the final decisions.

This involvement in the heavenly realms is still at the beginning stage because the reign of Christ and his people is eternal, it will last forever. God will show in the coming ages just how glorious and rich is the inheritance of Christ and his people. He has begun to do so today in the 'gospel age' which will last until Christ's second coming when the 'age of the new heavens and earth' will begin, during which God will reveal further glories.

Faith and works

For it is by grace you have been saved (verse 8). One of the most profound issues of the Protestant Reformation in the sixteenth century was the issue of the relationship between grace and merit. Grace is something we receive, not because we earn it but because, out of God's benevolence, he gives it to us as a gift. Merit, on the other hand, is a reward that is owed to someone for fulfilling the terms of a contract, or a legal agreement.

In the history of the Western church there had developed a rather complicated system of merit. The Roman Catholic Church made an important and fine distinction between two kinds of merit that are important to the life of the Christian. Those two kinds of merit were defined as condign merit (in Latin, *meritum decondigno*) and congruous merit (*meritum decongruo*). The distinction is as follows: condign merit is merit of such a degree that it obligates a just judge to render a reward. So if a person performs works of condign merit (and incidentally, Rome believes that it is within the power of Christian people to perform such works of condign merit), then this actually deserves a reward. God would be unjust not to reward it. Congruous merit, however, was seen as a lower order of merit. A good work may be performed that is not so virtuous as to impose an obligation upon God to reward it, but is virtuous enough to be congruous, or consistent with, or fitting, for God to bestow his favour toward it.

This distinction is significant for this reason: at the heart of the controversy that provoked the Protestant Reformation was the sacrament of penance. We all know the story of

Martin Luther and his objection to the way in which indulgences were being sold throughout Germany in an effort to raise funds for Rome. The peasants were being given the idea, because of the unscrupulous behaviour of a man by the name Tetzel, that they could buy forgiveness.

This was related to the sacrament of penance. The sacrament of penance is one of the seven sacraments of the Church of Rome, who define it as the 'special sacrament that is given to the church to aid those who have made shipwreck of their souls'. For Rome, justification takes place through the instrumental cause of baptism. Those baptised receive an infusion of justifying grace into their souls, and they remain in a state of grace, unless or until they commit a mortal sin. A mortal sin is called 'mortal' because it has the capacity to kill saving grace.

Members of the Roman Catholic communion go to church for confession. Confession is part of the sacrament of penance. Initial justification in Rome comes through baptism, but that justifying grace can be lost through the commission of mortal sin. If a person loses the grace of justification, they have to be justified again and the Roman Catholic Church, at the Council of Trent, defined the sacrament of penance as 'the second plank of justification for those who have made shipwreck of their faith'. In other words, the way back, the way of restoration to a state of grace after one has committed mortal sin, is through the sacrament of penance.

Now the sacrament of penance includes several parts, the first part of which is *sacramental confession*. The penitent comes to the church, goes into the confessional and confesses his sins in the hearing of the priest. There then follows priestly absolution where, in the name of Christ and through the power of the Church, the priest grants absolution. But the priest also gives to the penitent certain tasks to perform, tasks defined by Rome as 'works of satisfaction'.

There tends to be a different approach to and understanding of what repentance involves in Protestantism and Roman Catholicism. Roman Catholicism sees penance (or penitence and repentance) as an action that must be performed, including 'works of satisfaction'. These works of satisfaction include saying the rosary or going on a pilgrimage. In the sixteenth century one of the works of satisfaction that was authorised by the Church to meet the requirements of the sacrament of penance was the giving of alms. It was seen to be a virtuous thing to give donations to the poor, or to give one's money sacrificially to the work of the Church. Rome was very careful to insist that the giving of alms, in order for it to be pleasing to God, had to be done in the right spirit and not in the spirit of a crass, commercial transaction, by which the person was trying to buy for himself certain influence with the Almighty, or buy forgiveness for sins. So what was going on in Germany was, in fact, a corruption of what the Roman Catholic Church had actually taught with respect to indulgences.

When Luther sought to correct this corruption of the idea, he began to explore the whole concept of works of satisfaction. He noticed that Paul in Romans and here in Ephesians dashes to smithereens any claim to merit by the believer before the Living God, both condign and congruous. That is what the Reformation was all about: whether our justification is accomplished through a mixture of faith plus works, or by faith *alone*.

There are two unhelpful ways to think about the concept of grace. In respect of our simple definition of grace as *unmerited favour*, we have, firstly, a tendency to think of it somewhat abstractly. But really, grace is a personal act. It is something that God does. Grace is a Divine activity, it is an expression of graciousness. We experience assistance, favour, and benefits from the hands of God because he is gracious. If

God were not gracious then there would be no such thing as grace.

Secondly, we do have a tendency to think of grace almost as if it were some kind of quantity that could be augmented or diminished. We say, we have so much grace, that we grow in grace and the like. But Paul is using the term, *grace*, as the method or the basis by which we are saved.

In other words, Paul is setting forth the cause of our salvation. In the ancient world, Aristotle differentiated between several types of causes – what he called final causes, efficient causes, sufficient causes, formal causes and instrumental causes. It is sufficient for our purposes to define what is called the *instrumental cause* of something. The instrumental cause is defined as that by means of which something comes to pass. For example, if I want to pound a nail into a board: I with my strength am the efficient cause; the formal cause may be the blueprint I am trying to follow; the final cause is the purpose for which I am trying to fix something; but the instrumental cause in this case would be the hammer.

Now Rome defines the instrumental cause of justification as being the sacrament of baptism. If somebody is going to be justified, they are justified automatically, *ex opera operata*, through baptism. It is the instrumental cause of justification. Protestantism, on the other hand, says that the instrumental cause of justification, the means by which salvation is appropriated, the means by which we are brought into a saving relationship to Jesus Christ, is faith. The basis of it is grace. We are saved by grace through faith. Notice the absence of any consideration of merit. The source of our salvation is the grace of God. And the instrumental cause by which that salvation is appropriated is faith. **For it is by grace you have been saved, through faith – and this not from yourselves, it is the gift of God** (verse 8).

There has been an ongoing controversy on the structure of this verse. The question arises, what is the antecedent of 'this' or 'it' in the text where it says, 'by grace you have been saved, through faith – and *this* not from yourselves, *it* is the gift of God'. Does *this* refer to salvation? Or does *this* refer to faith? Is Paul saying that salvation is a gift of God? Or is he saying that faith itself is a gift of God?

Although Greek scholars argue about which of these is the preferred rendition of the Greek text, theologically it really doesn't matter. In both ways of reading that sentence, we have to come to the conclusion that faith is a gift of God. It is not an expression of human achievement, or of human effort, or of human ability. This is why every believer should be praising God daily for the fact that he has received as a gift not only the salvation that comes through faith, but the gift of faith itself.

If that were not enough to seal the controversy once and for all, Paul gives another qualifier here that no one should ever miss: **not by works, so that no-one can boast** (verse 9). I love that line from Augustus Toplady's great hymn, *Rock of Ages*: 'Nothing in my hand I bring, Simply to thy cross I cling.' The only merit that can get me into heaven is the merit of Jesus Christ. Paul says emphatically in Romans 3:20: 'No-one will be declared righteous in his sight by observing the law.' The Bible says explicitly that no-one will be justified through observing the law.

There is one more thing to be said before we leave this verse. Even though the apostle is teaching with crystal clarity the doctrine of justification by faith alone, he doesn't give any foundation for people adopting the so-called Antinomian heresy, which says that if justification is by faith alone, then all I have to do is believe and I am not required to perform good works. There is another formula of the Reformation: justification is by faith alone, but not by a faith that is alone.

What does this mean: not by a faith that is alone? It means that true faith will inevitably manifest itself in the performance of works of obedience.

The Roman Catholic formula for justification was this: faith plus works equals justification. The Reformation view of it was this: faith which leads to works equals justification. That is, if a person is justified, he is not justified on the basis of the works, by the works or through the works, but he is justified *to* the works. The performance of works are the result of faith and the fruit of justification. Notice how Paul ends this section: **For we are God's workmanship, created in Christ Jesus to do good works, which God prepared in advance for us to do** (verse 10). The purpose for which we have been chosen is to be conformed to the image of Christ, to be servants of God, to be people of obedience who live lives of godliness and righteousness.

4
Christian Unity
(2:11-22)

Therefore, remember that formerly you who are Gentiles by birth and called 'uncircumcised' by those who call themselves 'the circumcision' (that done in the body by the hands of men) — remember that at that time you were separate from Christ, excluded from citizenship in Israel and foreigners to the covenants of the promise, without hope and without God in the world. But now in Christ Jesus you who once were far away have been brought near through the blood of Christ.

For he himself is our peace, who has made the two one and has destroyed the barrier, the dividing wall of hostility, by abolishing in his flesh the law with its commandments and regulations. His purpose was to create in himself one new man out of the two, thus making peace, and in this one body to reconcile both of them to God through the cross, by which he put to death their hostility. He came and preached peace to you who were far away and peace to those who were near. For through him we both have access to the Father by one Spirit.

Consequently, you are no longer foreigners and aliens, but fellow-citizens with God's people and members of God's household, built on the foundation of the apostles and prophets, with Christ Jesus himself as the chief cornerstone. In him the whole building is joined together and rises to become a holy temple in the Lord. And in him you too are being built together to become a dwelling in which God lives by his Spirit.

Paul is asking his readers to think once more of what they were like prior to their conversion. My professor in Holland once said, 'Gentlemen, the essence of Christian theology is grace and the essence of Christian ethics is gratitude.' Somehow that pithy little statement has stayed with me and I have come back to it again and again in my thinking. We are not supposed to be motivated to godliness by fear of the consequences of breaking the law, but rather motivated by gratitude. Remember, Jesus said that the one who has been forgiven much, loves much.

In the Old Testament the root concept of apostasy was the idea of forgetting. As long as God's redemption was clear and fresh in the experience of the people, they were zealous in their worship and obedience. But as the memory of God's blessing faded, then their zeal began to fade as well. It is this link between memory and the motivating power of gratitude that produces the fruit of righteousness. Paul is reminding these Gentile converts that they are not to take for granted what God has done in them.

Therefore, remember that formerly you who are Gentiles by birth and called 'uncircumcised' by those who call themselves 'the circumcision' (that done in the body by the hands of men) -- remember that at that time you were separate from Christ, excluded from citizenship in Israel and foreigners to the covenants of the promise, without hope and without God in the world (verses 11,12).

This is a reference to the Old Testament ritual of circumcision that involved the cutting of the foreskin of the flesh from the male Jew. It was a theological sign, a sacred rite that was undertaken to seal the covenant God had made with his people. There is a sense in which the circumcised

59

were those who were cut off from the world, set apart, and consecrated to the special relationship of being in the family of God.

Those who were outside the sphere of this covenant of grace that God had made with Abraham and Moses were referred to as 'the uncircumcised'. Remember how David was outraged and horrified that his people would sit there and do nothing in the face of the mockery of Goliath (1 Samuel 17:36). What incensed David was that the challenge to the soldiers of Israel was coming from one who was uncircumcised. For to be uncircumcised was to be outside the sphere of God's redemptive favour.

The mark of Gentile Christians is not circumcision, but uncircumcision. They were once foreigners, or aliens, to the covenant of grace. The covenant of redemption is not their historic portion. They were separated from Christ, excluded from citizenship in Israel, and foreigners to the covenants of the promise. Paul climaxes this description by adding, 'without hope and without God in the world'.

I once talked to a man of Jewish origin who was very interested in dialogue among the great religions of the world. He was a man with a profound sense of compassion in humanitarian matters, and he was distressed by the fighting and the arguments that go on between members of various religions. I asked him, not out of a spirit of debate but out of a spirit of curiosity, what his private beliefs were. Among many things, he was convinced that we are called upon, as believers in God, to live ethical lives, to work for our fellowmen, and to seek to do what is right. Then he went on to say that he was sure there was no heaven or hell and that there was no alternative establishing of justice.

As I sat there and listened to him, much as I was drawn to his warmth, I felt very depressed that here was a man who was trying to remain committed to an ethic, to a high sense of virtue, without any hope of ultimate justice. Though I felt the attempt to be admirable, I thought it was foolish, because he had no hope for the future restoration of truth and justice.

When Paul refers to those who are without God in the world, he is describing pagan society. That is what we are when we are outside of a covenant relationship with God. Before I became a Christian, I was a pagan. I walked according to the lifestyles and the precepts and point of view of pagan America. We tend to use the softer term 'secular' rather than the term 'pagan', for we usually think of pagan countries as those with no historic conversion to Christianity, which are not part of the Judaeo-Christian culture. But what we have in America and the Western World is a post-Christian society.

But now in Christ Jesus you who once were far away have been brought near through the blood of Christ (verse 13). Paul uses a spatial image to describe the difference. In the past we were at a distance, but now we have been brought near and the means by which we have been brought near is the blood of Christ.

For he himself is our peace, who has made the two one and has destroyed the barrier, the dividing wall of hostility (verse 14). Paul has in view here the temple of Israel. In the temple there were areas that had their specific function. The heart of the temple was the Holy of Holies, where the throne of God was established and where the atonement was made on the Day of Atonement, once a year. The only human being that ever dared to enter the Holy of Holies was the high priest, and only after rigorous cleansing rites that prepared him for this once-a-year venture into the inside. Outside the Holy of Holies was the Holy Place to which there was access for believers. They could come that far and no further.

The wall of partition does not refer to the curtain that separated the Holy Place from the Holy of Holies. It is true that, at the moment of the atonement by Christ on the cross, the curtain which forbade access into the presence of God was removed once and for all. But Paul is referring to another barrier, the one that separated the Jew and the Gentile. The Gentiles could come into the Outer Court and no further, for there was a wall of partition that separated Gentiles from those who were full members in the covenant.

Abolishing in his flesh the law with its commandments and regulations (verse 15) does not mean that Jesus Christ has destroyed the law of God, but rather he performed in himself all of the requirements that had to be fulfilled for us to be reconciled to God. The reason why we have been estranged from God is because he is too holy to look upon our iniquity. We have violated God's law, and God has no fellowship with breakers of the law. We were estranged from him and there was no peace until the great armistice day of Calvary, when Jesus took upon himself the reality of the wrath of the Father. Christ won for us the rewards which were part of that covenant made with his people. At that point God offered a peace treaty to everyone who would put their trust in Christ. As Paul wrote in Romans 5:1, 'Since we have been justified through faith, we have peace with God.'

Jesus is called the Prince of peace not simply because he had the ability to arbitrate disputes between human beings and effect through his love and example reconciliation among estranged people; more importantly, he is the champion of peace between God and man. He is our peace because he made atonement by the shedding of his blood, and removed the distance that once separated us from God.

His purpose was to create in himself one new man out of the two, thus making peace, and in this one body to reconcile both of them to God through the cross, by which he put to death their hostility (verses 15, 16). To bring together not only God and man, but also Jew and Greek. I remember a conversation with my Jewish friend referred to earlier. His great fear of Christianity was the fear of anti-Semitism. He looked back to the terrible holocaust of World War II and to other periods in church history where those who were part of the Christian church used violence and bloodshed to express their anti-Semitism. Far from being apostles of peace between Jew and Christian, too often zealous members of the Christian church have become apostles of discord, hatred, and persecution.

Christ, while wanting us to be reconciled to God, also wants us to be reconciled to other people. The means of reconciling man to God, and man to man, is the same. It is by the cross that this hostility can be put to death. Jesus **came and preached peace to you who were far away and peace to those who were near. For through him we both have access to the Father by one Spirit** (verses 17, 18). Paul is not talking about a marriage between Judaism and Christianity, he is talking about Christians. Some were of Jewish origin and others of Gentile origin. Those who embrace Jesus Christ, whether they be Jew or Greek, slave or free, are now reconciled into one family, into one body, by their common devotion to Christ. He is our peace and our Redeemer.

Jew and Gentile together in the church

We see elsewhere in Paul's epistles, particularly in the book of Galatians, that one of the biggest issues in the first century Christian church was the question: What is the relationship between Jew and Gentile in the body of Christ?

There were those who wanted to look upon Gentiles as second-class citizens because they lacked the credentials of a long heritage tracing their religious history back to Abraham. Also, there was the fact that the Gentiles were not practitioners of the rigorous codes of dietary regulation and ritual observance that were such an integral part of the religious life of the nation of Israel. The greatest heresy that the first century church had to encounter was the Judaizing heresy that Paul deals with in Galatians. This heresy sought to impose upon Gentile converts to the Christian faith all of the dietary regulations and the ritual law of the Old Testament. It focused on the issue of circumcision. The Judaizing party insisted that any Gentile who joined the Christian church would have to be circumcised.

The first great ecclesiastical council of the Christian community was held in Jerusalem, and the record of it is found in Acts 15. Peter and Paul were involved and James, the brother of Jesus, was the presiding officer. The central issue at the council was the relationship between Jew and Gentile in the new covenant community. The basic spirit of the council of Jerusalem was to be as inclusive of the Gentile community as it could possibly be.

Now I give that background for this reason: Jesus' work of abolishing the law with its commandments and regulations could otherwise be open to serious misunderstanding. There is, in every generation, a constant threat to the church from a heresy called Antinomianism. The Antinomian heresy is the view that the law of God revealed in the Old Testament has nothing to do with the New Testament church; that the New Testament church is a church without law, a church that lives and breathes exclusively on the basis of grace (see on 2:9 above).

In Ephesians, Paul's emphasis is on the fact that salvation is by grace and not by the law. But the great danger that has always occurred when the doctrine of justification by faith alone has been preached, is the danger of thinking, 'All I have to do is believe in Christ and rely on the grace of God. I can then live any way I want, without any respect to the moral law of God.'

But the New Testament is far from abolishing God's

moral law. Jesus calls his disciples to obedience. He says, 'If you love me, you will obey what I command' (John 14:15). So what does Paul mean when he talks about Jesus abolishing or fulfilling the law along with its commandments and regulations?

The context points to a conflict that was historically real and vital between Jews and Gentiles. In Romans 2:12-15, Paul makes it clear that the moral law of God, revealed to Israel through Moses in the ten commandments, is revealed by the laws of nature to every Gentile. There is, therefore, a common basis for ethics to be found throughout the world. This natural law, reflected in the Decalogue, against stealing and murder and so on, people understand because the law is written on the human heart. So Paul is not saying that Christ abolished prohibitions against murder, stealing, or anything similar. He is referring to the regulations and specific commandments of the Old Testament law that were delivered to Jews as Jews.

This included the strict regimen of dietary regulations that God gave to Israel. God's reason for the Jewish people maintaining a scrupulous, unique set of dietary principles was not simply health or nutrition. Rather, God was creating a nation that was set apart from all other nations down to what appeared, on the surface at least, to be matters of minutiae.

In addition to that, there were strict codes that were commanded by God in terms of the sacrificial system of worship, such as the Day of Atonement and the offering of sacrifices on the altar. This is explained in the New Testament as God's way of foreshadowing the supreme event yet to come that would fulfil what the Old Testament ritual symbolised. The sacrifice of bulls on the altar in the Old Testament did not have the power or the efficacy in and of itself to atone for sins. The value of these sacrifices was in a symbolic foreshadowing of the perfect sacrifice that would be offered once and for all by Christ. Of course, once the real sacrifice has been made, it would be an insult to his finished work and to the perfection of his atonement to continue those shadows or symbols. So the New Testament argument is that once the perfect sacrifice is made, then all of the Old Testament practices that looked forward to the perfect sacrifice were finished. It wasn't as if the sacrifice of Christ contradicted the Old Testament regulations in connection with sin offerings and that they were abolished in the sense of the earlier rules being wrong. Jesus never corrects the Old Testament law, he fulfils it. There is a serious difference here between correcting and fulfilling.

What about Jesus' teaching in the Sermon on the Mount, when he says, "You have heard that it was said, 'Eye for eye, and tooth for tooth.' But I tell you, Do not resist an evil person. If someone strikes you on the right cheek, turn to him the other also" (Matthew 5:38, 39 and so on). On the surface it seems as if Jesus is correcting the law of Moses. That was not the spirit of Jesus' teaching regarding the law. He had utmost respect for the law of Moses and constantly, in his debates with the Pharisees, the Sadducees, and the scribes, he tried to settle his arguments with them simply by an appeal to the law. Even when Satan tried to get him to do things that were contrary to the will of God, Jesus referred to the law delivered by Moses. Now when Jesus appealed to the Old Testament literature, his favourite phrase was a technical term in the Jewish vocabulary that every Jew understood. The phrase, 'It is written ...' clearly refers to the sacred Scriptures of the Old Testament. It is exactly the same as if he said to them, 'The Bible says ...'.

Now, just as the phrase, 'It is written' carried a unique meaning to the Jews, so did the phrase 'It was said'. The difference is between written law and spoken law. To the first century Jew, that was the difference between the writings of sacred Scripture and what was called the Holoka, the oral tradition of the rabbis. What the rabbinic tradition did was to interpret the writings of sacred Scripture and set down traditions that were then passed on from generation to generation. When Jesus opposes a tradition, he is being sharply critical of those who have substituted the tradition of men for the law of God. I think it is clear in the Sermon on the Mount, that when Jesus said, 'You have heard that it was said, Eye for eye and tooth for tooth,' he was not being critical about an eye for an eye and a tooth for a tooth, but rather about the harsh and severe way in which the rabbis interpreted and applied the Old Testament law. That is, Jesus' quarrel was not with the Old Testament, it was with the contemporary traditions of the theologians of his day.

The legislation of diet, the legislation of ritual for the sacrificial system and the traditions of the Jews became serious barriers of communication with Gentiles. The Gentiles didn't want any part of the dietary law, or the sacrificial system, or the traditions that were set down by the rabbis. Jesus **himself is our peace, who has made the two one and has destroyed the barrier, the dividing wall of hostility** (verse 14) by fulfilling the Old Testament law. He doesn't annul the moral law, but he fulfils the dietary laws, the sacrificial laws, and he puts aside the human traditions that were barriers to union among his people. So **he came and preached peace to you who were far away** (Gentiles) **and peace to those who were near** (Jews). Peace to the Jew and peace to the Gentile.

For through him we both have access to the Father by one Spirit. Notice that access is given to Jew and Gentile into the family of God, so that Jew and Gentile Christians both say, 'Abba,' to the same Person, by the Holy Spirit. They are both adopted into the family of God.

Consequently, you (Gentiles) **are no longer foreigners**

and aliens, but fellow-citizens with God's people and members of God's household (verse 19). Paul is not describing and defining what a local congregation looks like, but rather he is developing and revealing to us something of the mystical body of Christ. The church is the people of God, made up of both Jews and Gentiles who are adopted into the family of God.

Apostles and prophets

In addition to the metaphor of the family, Paul develops the metaphor of a building. So often today we think of a church as a building, made out of stone or bricks and mortar, when rather the church is the people. Yet here Paul uses the illustration of a building to describe the nature of the church. And this illustration has been an occasion for much controversy: **built on the foundation of the apostles and prophets, with Christ Jesus himself as the chief cornerstone** (verse 20). As mentioned in the Introduction, some people have raised questions about whether or not Ephesians was written by Paul, because Paul normally refers to Jesus as the foundation of the church, and here he refers to the prophets and the apostles as the foundation of the church.

There is further controversy at this point. Some commentators believe Paul to be saying that the New Testament church is established on the foundation of the New Testament apostles and the New Testament prophets like Agabus and the rest. But Scripture as a whole would not support such a view. For example, in the book of Revelation we see the structure of the New Jerusalem, which honours both the prophets of the Old Testament and the apostles of the New Testament (21:12-14). It is clear that what Paul is saying here is that the foundation of this new edifice is the prophets of the Old Testament and the apostles of the New Testament.

The apostles of the New Testament correspond in their vocation to the prophets of the Old Testament. The prophets of the Old Testament and the apostles of the New Testament were both divinely chosen, divinely called, divinely commissioned, divinely gifted, and divinely inspired agents of revelation. They were the spokesmen for God. The foundational authority for the New Testament community is vested in those to whom Jesus gave authority to be his spokesmen.

But why isn't Jesus called the foundation here? In case we think that the apostles and prophets are given a place of pre-eminence above Jesus, we need to read this text carefully, especially where it says that Jesus is the chief cornerstone. The cornerstone in contemporary building is often a brick containing mementos that will be cemented in place at an opening ceremony; it is for cosmetic value and has no structural significance. But the stone that is being described here has its roots in ancient masonry. It was the brick by which the builder lined up the whole building. Often it was the first brick to be laid. It was the keystone for the whole building – pull this brick out and everything falls. So the foundation was laid in and upon the chief cornerstone.

The full metaphor is that the foundation of the prophets and the apostles is the base that rests ultimately upon the chief cornerstone, the keystone of the whole structure, who is Christ. Therefore, the authority of both prophet and apostle is derived from the chief keystone of the church, Christ.

At the same time, however, this passage gives extraordinary significance to the prophets and the apostles. This is something to notice in a day and age when it is commonplace to hear people say, 'Jesus I believe, but it is the apostle Paul I can't handle,' or, 'I don't want to listen to the apostles, but Jesus is the authority for me.' To say that, is to deny the authority of Christ, because Christ is the one who appointed the apostles saying that those who receive them receive him. Those who reject the apostles reject Christ.

In him the whole building is joined together and rises to become a holy temple in the Lord. And in him you too are being built together to become a dwelling in which God lives by his Spirit (verse 21, 22). Notice, he is referring not only to the whole congregation of Jews and Gentiles added together, but to every individual believer. He is showing that the individual believer is a person in whom God the Holy Spirit dwells. Elsewhere, Paul says that our bodies are the temple of God (2 Corinthians 6:16). Just as God dwelt by his Spirit in the temple in the Old Testament, so now he dwells in us. That is so significant in the dispute between Jew and Gentile because the Jew could not look at the Gentile convert and regard him as second-class. The Jewish believer has to look at the Gentile convert and recognise the indwelling Holy Spirit.

5
The Ministry of Paul
(3:1-13)

For this reason I, Paul, the prisoner of Christ Jesus for the sake of you Gentiles —

Surely you have heard about the administration of God's grace that was given to me for you, that is, the mystery made known to me by revelation, as I have already written briefly. In reading this, then, you will be able to understand my insight into the mystery of Christ, which was not made known to men in other generations as it has now been revealed by the Spirit to God's holy apostles and prophets. This mystery is that through the gospel the Gentiles are heirs together with Israel, members together of one body, and sharers together in the promise in Christ Jesus.

I became a servant of this gospel by the gift of God's grace given me through the working of his power. Although I am less than the least of all God's people, this grace was given me: to preach to the Gentiles the unsearchable riches of Christ, and to make plain to everyone the administration of this mystery, which for ages past was kept hidden in God, who created all things. His intent was that now, through the church, the manifold wisdom of God should be made known to the rulers and authorities in the heavenly realms, according to his eternal purpose which he accomplished in Christ Jesus our Lord. In him and through faith in him we may approach God with freedom and confidence. I ask you, therefore, not to be discouraged because of my sufferings for you, which are your glory.

The bulk of Ephesians chapter 3 is comprised of material that one almost never hears sermons preached from in our day, except for those who are preaching through the book and cannot avoid the subject matter that is found here. The central theme of the third chapter is the importance of the role of the Gentiles in the early Christian community and is directly related to the special commission that God gave Paul in his apostolic ministry. The reason why we rarely hear sermons from the third chapter of Ephesians is that in the twentieth century it is universally taken for granted, without any dispute or controversy, that the Christian Church is open to people from all different nationalities and ethnic backgrounds.

If we put ourselves in the position of the original recipients of this epistle, however, we begin to get a taste of the sense of drama and stirring emotion that this chapter must have provoked in its original audience. It is possible that the people who read the original letter to the Ephesians found chapter 3 to be the most provocative section of the whole epistle. What sparked the most interest among them was Paul's elaborate comments that are found here in the third chapter regarding the inclusion of the Gentiles in the body of Christ.

In addition to that theme, there is in chapter 3 some important information that is of abiding interest to us and to future generations of Christians concerning the personal character of the apostle himself. This is obviously the most personal dimension to be found in a letter that we believe to be a cyclical letter, not the normal kind that Paul would send to his friends in the churches. Here we get a glimpse into Paul's character and self-understanding in respect of who he was, what his task was, what his passion was, and what was his mission. For that reason, it remains of abiding significance to the Christian community.

In fact, there are such interesting personal elements in this third chapter that some who have challenged the Pauline authorship of Ephesians have argued that it represents an attempt by the anonymous writer to pass off this letter as being genuinely Pauline. This unknown writer, they say, wrote the third chapter as an afterthought in order to convince his readers that indeed it did come from the apostle Paul.

We notice that, in the first verse, Paul identifies himself by name as the author of this epistle: **For this reason I, Paul, the prisoner of Christ Jesus for the sake of you Gentiles**. Notice how Paul describes himself here. There's a wonderful irony in the words that he chooses. He calls himself 'a prisoner of Christ Jesus'. Now the irony here is that Paul is writing this epistle from a Roman prison, under the authority of the emperor of Rome whose name was Nero. But rather than identifying himself as, 'I, Paul, a prisoner of Nero, the emperor of Rome,' he glories in his incarceration under the lordship of Christ. He sees himself not as being held and bound by the fetters of Rome, but rather as being held and mastered by the Lord Jesus Christ.

Down in verse 7, he says, **I became a servant of this gospel by the gift of God's grace**. He uses two words then to describe himself and his mission: he is a 'prisoner' and he is a 'servant'. This is consistent with what the apostle says of himself in his other epistles. He frequently identifies himself as the slave of Jesus Christ, one who has been purchased, who has been bought at a price, who is the possession of Christ. He stresses the fact of having been in bondage to sin and set at liberty by the redemption that came through Christ. He affirms that one is not free until one becomes imprisoned by the Master who is Jesus.

Paul reveals his personal self-understanding in this image of the prisoner and the servant. There is a reason why he is held captive by Jesus: **for the sake of you Gentiles**. The New

Testament gives great importance to the role of the apostles following upon their selection and commission by Jesus. The word *apostolos* means 'one who has been sent'. An apostle is an ambassador or an emissary for an authority figure such as a king or a prime minister. He spoke with the authority of the one who commissioned him. The first apostle in the New Testament is Jesus himself. His office is to be the Anointed One sent by and from the Father. Jesus says: 'When you have lifted up the Son of Man, then you will know who I am and that I do nothing on my own but speak just what the Father has taught me' (John 8:28). When Jesus commissioned his apostles, he declared to them, 'He who receives you receives me, and he who receives me receives the one who sent me' (Matthew 10:40).

A very important saint who lived at the beginning of the second century, Ignatius of Antioch in Syria, wrote several letters to the Christian churches in Asia Minor, as well as to Rome. In writing his letter to the Romans, he said, 'I do not order you as Peter or Paul, for I am not an apostle, but I am a convict.' It is interesting that Ignatius can call himself a prisoner but not an apostle. Paul calls himself an apostle but also a prisoner. So even Ignatius, one of the early church fathers, and others such as Clement, understood that there was a line of demarcation between their authority and that of their predecessors, the apostles, who were called directly and immediately by Christ.

And yet, as we read the New Testament, we discover that there is something different about Paul, that sets him apart from the other apostles. In particular, there was much controversy attached to the question of his legitimacy as an apostle because he wasn't one of the twelve disciples, and had not been an eye-witness of the resurrection. Rather, he was called directly by Jesus on the road to Damascus. The legitimacy and authenticity of Paul's apostolic credentials were confirmed by the other apostles. But Paul had a special task, a special mission to perform, for he was designated the apostle to the Gentiles.

So, as he discusses this question of the role of the Gentiles in the body of Christ, Paul is speaking of something that is very close to his own heart. That is why, instead of ministering in and around Jerusalem, Paul made three very difficult, arduous, and lengthy missionary journeys, as recorded in the Book of Acts. He spent his life fulfilling this commission to be the apostle to the Gentiles, going to different places, spreading the Christian faith and establishing Christian churches. Paul is not only the greatest theologian in the history of the Christian church, he is also the greatest evangelist in the history of the Christian church.

Surely you have heard about the administration of God's grace that was given to me for you, that is, the mystery made known to me by revelation (verses 2-3). Paul was selected to be a special object of Divine favour and grace, so that he might impart the gospel to the Gentiles. It has been mentioned already that the term *mystery* does not mean a secret which remains an enigma to us. Rather, it refers to something which was always in the plan of God but which had been obscured in the earlier chapters of redemptive history. But God revealed this mystery to Paul:

> **the mystery made known to me by revelation, as I have already written briefly. In reading this, then, you will be able to understand my insight into the mystery of Christ, which was not made known to men in other generations as it has now been revealed by the Spirit to God's holy apostles and prophets. This mystery is that through the gospel the Gentiles are heirs together with Israel, members together of one body, and sharers together in the promise in Christ Jesus** (verses 3-6).

All people, from all nations, who profess Jesus as Lord and Saviour become incorporated into his mystical body, the church, and participate in the legacy of the Saviour. All are heirs of God, together with Christ (Romans 8:17).

Paul says that this revelation by the Spirit is to God's holy apostles and prophets. There is something strange. Usually, when the apostle speaks of prophets and apostles, he does it in that order, prophets and apostles. When in that order, the prophets obviously refer to the Old Testament men whom we know as the prophets of God. Remember that in the Old Testament a prophet was a spokesman for God, through whom God revealed his special truth. The office in the New Testament that corresponds to the office of prophet in the Old Testament is the office of apostle.

In this instance, however, Paul reverses the order and speaks of God's holy apostles and prophets, which makes some commentators think that Paul is referring to others in the apostolic entourage who are not at the level of apostles, but who have the gift of prophecy, men like Agabus who is mentioned in the book of Acts. Another possibility is that Paul is using a double phrase, saying that those who are apostles are also prophets. In either case, Paul describes the apostles here as being 'holy'.

Some critics have used this to suggest that Paul did not write Ephesians because the apostle Paul would never boast by calling himself 'holy'. In reply, it must be said that throughout the writings of Paul, while he expresses again and again his personal humility, he is also repeatedly and consistently firm in calling attention to the importance of the office he holds. Although he minimises his personal merit and worth, nevertheless he magnifies his office as an apostle. He understood that the office of the apostle was special. The word 'holy' here does not mean 'pure', it means 'set apart' or 'consecrated'.

We see the same contrast in verse 7 between Paul's minimising of his own personal character and yet at the same time calling attention to the sober importance of the office of apostle that he bears. He says, **I became a servant of this gospel** (a humble statement) **by the gift of God's grace given me through the working of his power.** Paul recognises that he is a servant, and that even this servitude is a gift from God, given to him through the working of God's power, not of his own. He is quick to qualify this by adding, **Although I am less than the least of all God's people, this grace was given me**.

If words mean anything, it is impossible for anyone or anything to be less than the least. This is like saying you are higher than the highest. But Paul uses this hyperbolic phrase to stress, in such a way that his readers can't miss it, that he has not merited this position or this authority; he has received it by the grace of God. If there is any statement in the book of Ephesians that carries the unmistakable signature of Paul the apostle, it is this one. He calls himself elsewhere, 'the worst of all sinners' (1 Timothy 1:15).

If Paul had anything in his character that distinguished him, it was his genuine humility. He really was aware of his dependence on the grace of God. But the fact that he was less than the least does not cancel out the significance of his message. **This grace was given me: to preach to the Gentiles, the unsearchable riches of Christ** (verse 8). To be a minister in any capacity in the kingdom of God is to carry a treasure in earthen vessels. There is not one of us who is qualified for this task in terms of his own righteousness, purity or integrity, because the message that we preach is beyond estimation in terms of its value. Paul says that he was called **to make plain to everyone the administration of this mystery, which for ages past was kept hidden in God, who created all things** (verse 9).

God's intent was that through the ministry and mission of the church, **the manifold wisdom of God should be made known to the rulers and authorities in the heavenly**

realms. Paul is saying that this mystery is revealed to the apostles to be expressed and taught to men. But even angels and demons did not know of this secret counsel of God. So it is to be made known to the powers and principalities, and to angels. It is the task of the church to make God's plan of salvation plain to the whole cosmos, even to the heavenly beings. This is **according to his eternal purpose which he accomplished in Christ Jesus our Lord**. Because of this, Paul says, **I ask you, therefore, not to be discouraged because of my sufferings for you, which are your glory**.

God's purpose, like his decrees, stands from all eternity. In the covenant of redemption made by the Father and the Son the plan for the elect's salvation was ratified. Throughout all subsequent history there has not been, nor could there be, a shadow of turning or an alteration, no matter however slight. Notice the past tense of 'accomplished'; this is a finished work, a completed atonement. God was well pleased with the faithful obedience unto death of Jesus Christ. His pleasure is so full that nothing we do can add or detract from it. Jesus testified to this completed work when, upon the cross, he cried out, 'It is finished!'

Only those whose confidence is in the sovereignty of God in the redemption of the elect could be admonished not to lose heart or grow discouraged at the thought of the Apostle Paul imprisoned for the faith. He therefore admonishes them not to faint at his tribulations. In fact, he says, 'Rejoice, this is your glory.' The apostle was proving himself faithful through trials, even as Jesus had done. God was well pleased with Paul too, because he was showing forth the sufferings of Christ (Colossians 1:24). This was also part of that eternal plan and purpose of God which was being perfectly unfolded before their eyes. Discouragement with the outworkings of the plan of God is simply inconsistent with a bold confession of God as sovereign and Christ as reigning Lord.

6
Paul's Second Prayer for his Readers (3:14-21)

For this reason I kneel before the Father, from whom his whole family in heaven and on earth derives its name. I pray that out of his glorious riches he may strengthen you with power through his Spirit in your inner being, so that Christ may dwell in your hearts through faith. And I pray that you, being rooted and established in love, may have power, together with all the saints, to grasp how wide and long and high and deep is the love of Christ, and to know this love that surpasses knowledge — that you may be filled to the measure of all the fulness of God.

Now to him who is able to do immeasurably more than all we ask or imagine, according to his power that is at work within us, to him be glory in the church and in Christ Jesus throughout all generations, for ever and ever! Amen.

For this reason I kneel before the Father. Commentators are divided on how to understand what Paul is saying here. Is he, by using the term 'kneel', referring to his sense of wanting to be on his face in a posture of homage and obeisance before the Kingship of God? Or does he speak of kneeling in the sense of assuming a posture of prayer? The commentators are divided for this reason: the way in which Jewish people prayed at that time was by standing and looking up into heaven. There are, however, instances recorded in the Old Testament and in the New when people do kneel in a posture of prayer. In either case, the basic import remains the same.

He continues, **from whom his whole family in heaven and on earth derives its name** (verse 15). The problem the translator has with this verse is that we have nothing in our English language which captures the play on words here in the Greek text. The term that is translated 'family', is the Greek word *patria*, and it refers to all of the descendants of a particular patriarch. In one sense, the whole Jewish nation could be traced back to Abraham and be called the *patria* of Abraham. It does not just refer to the single family unit as in our own culture.

Does **his whole family in heaven and on earth** refer to the elect family of God, namely the church universal, or is this an allusion to the universal Fatherhood of God, as creator of all human beings? There is a difficulty here in determining which of these is meant. In the context, it makes more sense to read it as the NIV does, namely, referring to the family of God. This family of God incorporates those who are in heaven, as well as those who are on earth.

Another question is this: when Paul speaks about heavenly members of the family of God, is he perhaps referring to the angelic host that are a part of the cohort of God that serve him in heaven? Angels are called 'sons of God' from time to time in the Scripture and perhaps that is what Paul has in mind. Remember that, throughout this epistle, Paul keeps drawing our attention away from this world to the heavenly places, to the abode of the powers and the principalities, of the angels and of the risen and exalted Christ.

Or perhaps the apostle here, by referring to members of the family of God who are in heaven, is giving us a seminal introduction to a doctrine that became an important part of the Apostles' Creed: 'I believe in the communion of the saints.' That is, the Church of Jesus Christ includes in its membership believers from all tribes, all nations and all times, and that we have a mystical fellowship not only with those brothers and sisters in the Lord who are alive and within the scope of our acquaintanceship, but with those who are living right now all over the world, and not only with those who are alive now, but with those who have gone to heaven.

That may seem a little bizarre, but look at it from this perspective. To be a Christian is to be in Christ and Christ to be in me. Every Christian, therefore, is in a mystical union with Jesus. When we die and go to heaven, that mystical union is not broken. Nothing can separate us from the union that we have with Jesus. If anything, our union with Christ is enhanced and intensified after death. So it is a very simple equation: if presently I am alive and have a saving relationship with Jesus, I am in mystical union with him. Insofar as I am united to him, I am also in mystical union with everybody else who is likewise united with him. Our unity with all saints living and dead is through our Saviour himself (see further discussion of this important theme at the end of this section, beginning on page 88).

We don't know whether Paul, by speaking of the heavenly members of the family of God, is referring to angels or to the departed saints. In any case, Paul says, **I pray that out of his** (God's) **glorious riches he may strengthen you with power**

through his Spirit in your inner being, so that Christ may dwell in your hearts through faith (verses 16, 17a). I remember a little tract that became very famous in the Christian world called 'My Heart, Christ's Home'. We hear frequently in the language of Christians sentiments like this: 'Have you asked Christ into your heart? Is Jesus in your heart?' It is such a commonplace Christian idea, so widely discussed and mentioned in our heritage, that you may find it astonishing to discover that this is the only place in the whole Bible that mentions Christ dwelling in our hearts. I think that the idea is repeated whenever Paul speaks of Christ in us and we in him. But he doesn't locate it specifically in the heart anywhere else but here.

What he is getting at, obviously, is that when a person becomes a Christian and has authentic faith, he has a real mystical union with Christ, so that Christ really comes to indwell the believer. When we exercise faith in Jesus Christ, his righteousness is counted towards us and we are justified. At that same moment, Christ, by virtue of the Holy Spirit, comes to dwell inside of us.

Paul chooses to use two different phrases. He speaks first of all about our innermost being and then goes on to describe it in terms of the heart. Even though this is the only place in the New Testament where we have a description of Jesus dwelling in our hearts, it is certainly not the only place in the New Testament where the heart is used to describe the innermost centre of human life.

I pray that out of his glorious riches he may strengthen you with power through his Spirit in your inner being. Whatever spiritual power they have, Paul is praying that it will increase so that it will permeate the very depth of their being. **So that Christ may dwell in your hearts through faith**. Christ should live, not at the periphery, but at the very centre of their life.

And I pray that you, being rooted and established in love, may have power, together with all the saints, to grasp how wide and long and high and deep is the love of Christ (verses 17,18). The form of these verbs indicates past action that has taken place and is continuing. The apostle is mixing his metaphors, drawing one from agriculture (rooted) and the other from masonry or the building industry (established or founded). He is asking that those who have been rooted and established in the love of God might not be impotent, but that they might have the power to accomplish something. He is praying that our understanding will be able to penetrate one of the great mysteries. It is not enough that we understand God to be loving, nor that we understand there to be a love that belongs to Christ. We need divine power to have a deeper understanding of the dimensions of the love of Christ.

We normally talk in terms of three dimensions. Paul gives us four, but why he chooses to do it this way, he doesn't tell us. He wants believers to be able to understand the love of Christ completely and **to know this love that surpasses knowledge – that you may be filled to the measure of all the fullness of God** (verse 19). Do you want everything that God has for you, the full measure of his grace? If you are going to achieve full stature in the Christian life, you need to be filled with the love of Christ, a love that surpasses understanding and knowledge. It is not that it is apart from knowledge, it is not that it is against knowledge, but it goes beyond the head and comes into the heart.

Paul then gives a benediction in the middle of the epistle. It is as though he says, 'I am finished with this theme, I am going to turn my attention now to the practical applications of this depth and riches of the mystery of Christ's love in the family of God.' So he says: **Now to him who is able to do immeasurably more** (literally, far, far more) **than all we**

ask or imagine, according to his power that is at work within us, to him be glory in the church and in Christ Jesus throughout all generations, for ever and ever! Amen.

The locus of God's glory is in his church, the Bride of Christ. Throughout history, but especially in our day and particularly in the evangelical church, people attempt to displace this glory elsewhere. Heed Paul's insistence: 'to him be glory in the church.' God will share his glory with no man, no institution, no para-church ministry. The Bride of Christ, however, will be so fully adorned with grace, beauty, truth, love, mercy and righteousness that her glory will be incomparable. To whom do you ascribe glory?

Throughout the benediction Paul employs a vocabulary and repetition that is artfully designed to cause wonder and amazement. It is a hyperbole that still falls short of truly expressing how immeasurable is the work of God. In a sense there can be no exaggeration of how much God is prepared to do for his church, nor for how long; 'for ever and ever' he will glorify her.

From verse 14 through to verse 21, there is an interlude of prayer. It is a prayer of thanksgiving, it is a prayer of adoration and it is a prayer of apostolic intercession for the saints that they may grow in their capacity to be filled with the love of Christ. This prayer prepares us for the grand theme that Paul is going to expound in chapter 4, which has to do with the unity of the body of Christ, the church.

The communion of the saints

A major theme of Ephesians is the unfolding of the nature of the church. Paul puts stress on the unity of believers in Christ effected by the Holy Spirit. The New Testament makes use of various concepts, images, analogies, and metaphors to describe this union. The church is called the 'Body of Christ,' the 'People of God,' the 'Family of God,' the 'Building of God,' to name a few. Here we see images drawn from the physical body, from building construction, and from the earthly family.

One affirmation found in the Apostles' Creed is this: 'I believe in the communion of saints.' This confession of faith is often misunderstood to mean, 'I believe in the Lord's Supper.' Since the Lord's Supper is often called 'Holy Communion', it is easy to leap to the conclusion that the communion of saints is just another phrase for the Lord's Supper. Although the communion of saints is certainly closely related to the sacrament of the Lord's Supper, the two are not identical.

The communion of saints refers to the church of Christ. More specifically, we should refer to the 'invisible church'. The invisible church refers to those persons who are truly redeemed, truly regenerate and spiritually united with Christ. The invisible church is distinguished from the visible church because no man can read another person's heart. We look on the outward appearance, but God alone can read the heart. The visible church refers to the institution called 'the church' that has visible participants whose names appear on the roll of a local congregation. In most churches anyone who makes an outward profession of faith (and meets other criteria for membership) is admitted to active fellowship in the visible church.

There is, however, a crucial difference between a profession of faith and the possession of faith. James labours the point that it is not the mere claim to faith that makes us Christians. We must have what we claim to have to be truly in Christ. Jesus sombrely warned about those who say, 'Lord, Lord,' who are not his (Matthew 7:21). He made it clear that people can honour him with their lips while their hearts are far from him. The visible church contains weeds among the wheat, unbelievers co-existing alongside believers (Matthew 13:24-30). The church is, as Augustine called it, a *corpus per mixtum*, a mixed body.

The invisible church, though distinguished from the visible church, is not a separate institution that exists outside the visible church. Though on rare occasions (for various reasons) a person who is truly regenerate may not be a member of a visible church, it must be said that the invisible church exists substantially within the visible church.

There are those, particularly in our day, who are so disenchanted with the visible church that they steadfastly refuse to join any local visible church. Such a posture is misguided and involves overt disobedience to the commands of Christ. Though it is possible for a believer to be confused about this for a season, someone who persists in such a posture is, in all probability, not a believer. It is the duty of every Christian to join a visible church.

The invisible church includes all those who enjoy a mystical union with Christ. To be a Christian is to be 'in Christ' and to have Christ 'in you'.

This mystical union is set forth in the New Testament by way of five comparisons. It is likened to:

(1) the union of a vine with its branches or an olive tree and its limbs (John 15:1-10; Romans 11:17-24);

(2) the union of the Father and the Son, indicating a sweet accord and harmony (John 17:20-23);

(3) the union between the Head and the body (Ephesians 4:15-16);

(4) the union between a husband and wife – the church is the bride of Christ (Ephesians 5:22-33);

(5) the union of the stones in a building with the Chief Cornerstone that sustains the others (Ephesians 2:19-22; 1 Peter 2:4-8).

Robert Dabney speaks of a threefold union between the believer and Christ. The first is a legal union. In our justification God imputes the righteousness of Christ to us. This forensic declaration applies the merits of Christ to the sinner's ledger before the tribunal of God.

The second is a spiritual union by which the indwelling Holy Spirit effects changes within us. It yields spiritual life (vitality) in our souls.

The third is the communion of saints. Every soul that is spiritually united to Christ is thereby united with every other soul that is in union with him. We have fellowship not only with Christ and with our contemporaries but also with every other believer who has ever lived. Our union with Christ lasts forever. At this moment, as I enjoy spiritual communion with Christ, I have spiritual fellowship with all who are his, both past and present.

Union and communion

When we speak of spiritual union or mystical union with Christ, we must be careful not to fall into heretical forms of mysticism. In Eastern forms of mysticism the religious goal is a kind of unity (*unio*) with the deity by which the individual is so absorbed by the 'ultimate one' that personal identity is obliterated. In Christian mystical union, the self is not lost or erased by being merged with some oversoul or universal essence.

The second heresy that has re-emerged in some strands of modern evangelicalism (though by virtue of the presence of this heresy the advocates of it are not entitled to the term evangelical) is that of *apotheosis*. In *apotheosis* the believer is said to be so united to Christ that a kind of deification of the believer takes place. I have read one advocate of this position who said, 'By virtue of the indwelling Holy Spirit the believer is no less the incarnation of God than Jesus was.'

It is because of these heresies that the church prefers to stress the word 'communion'. The word 'communion' has the prefix *com*, which means 'with'. When we are united with Christ and with each other, our personal identities remain intact, though sweetly and profoundly enriched by the spiritual fellowship we enjoy.

7
The Body of Christ
(4:1-16)

As a prisoner for the Lord, then, I urge you to live a life worthy of the calling you have received. Be completely humble and gentle; be patient, bearing with one another in love. Make every effort to keep the unity of the Spirit through the bond of peace. There is one body and one Spirit — just as you were called to one hope when you were called — one Lord, one faith, one baptism; one God and Father of all, who is over all and through all and in all.

But to each one of us grace has been given as Christ apportioned it. This is why it says: "When he ascended on high, he led captives in his train and gave gifts to men." (What does "he ascended" mean except that he also descended to the lower, earthly regions? He who descended is the very one who ascended higher than all the heavens, in order to fill the whole universe.) It was he who gave some to be apostles, some to be prophets, some to be evangelists, and some to be pastors and teachers, to prepare God's people for works of service, so that the body of Christ may be built up until we all reach unity in the faith and in the knowledge of the Son of God and become mature, attaining to the whole measure of the fulness of Christ.

Then we will no longer be infants, tossed back and forth by the waves, and blown here and there by every wind of teaching and by the cunning and craftiness of men in their deceitful scheming. Instead, speaking the truth in love, we will in all things grow up into him who is the Head, that is, Christ. From him the whole body, joined and held together by every supporting ligament, grows and builds itself up in love, as each part does its work.

As a prisoner for the Lord, then, I urge you to live a life worthy of the calling you have received. To be called by God out of the world and into the body of Christ is the highest vocation possible. The Greek word for church, *ecclesia*, is made up of a prefix and a root. The prefix is *ek* – out of. The root is the verb *coleo*, to call. The church in the New Testament is made up of those who are called out from the world, from darkness, from damnation, from paganism, to become members of the body of Christ.

Paul is not saying that they were called out of the world because they were worthy. He has already stressed the point that the calling by which we are made the children of God is utterly gracious. But after God calls us to be his children, and in response to that unspeakable gift, we should endeavour to do everything in our power to live lives that are worthy of our calling. What motivates and stimulates our behaviour in attempting to live worthy lives is the grace by which we have been saved.

But what does it mean to live a life worthy of our calling? **Be completely humble and gentle; be patient, bearing with one another in love. Make every effort to keep the unity of the Spirit through the bond of peace** (verses 2, 3).

In the life of the church we often regard behavioural standards as the marks of spirituality, whereas these are often superficial substitutes for the virtues that the New Testament sets forth as the real touchstones of piety and godliness. There is a close relationship between the virtues that the apostle lists here and what elsewhere is described as the 'fruit of the Holy Spirit' (Galatians 5:22, 23). These particular virtues are intangible, difficult to measure and not nearly as obvious as surface behavioural forms. Yet they represent the real presence of grace in a person's life.

Look at them again: **Be completely humble and gentle**. When I am doing seminars on marriage, I will ask women in the group what virtues or characteristics they most desire to find in men. No matter how many times I have asked that question nor how many groups I have put it before, the answers tend to be the same. At the top of the list there is a strange combination. What they want from men are basically three things: confidence, strength and tenderness. I think that *tenderness* is a critical word that puts restraints on the other two qualities. Somebody who mixes strength with tenderness is a person who will never abuse strength in the direction of brutality.

The women also say that they want men who have a spirit of confidence. Again, there is a link between strength, confidence and tenderness. A person who is strong and confident of his strength can afford to be tender. There is a tremendous difference between confidence and arrogance. Arrogance seeks to humiliate other people. The arrogant person expresses a kind of disdain or contempt for other people, and nothing is more destructive to the harmony of a group or a marriage. A marriage is a relationship of two people. The church follows the paradigm of that marriage relationship, and the virtues that are necessary for a successful marriage are the same virtues that are necessary for the success of any interpersonal relationships, particularly interpersonal relationships within a church.

So that when the apostle says that humility and gentleness are to be manifested as being worthy of the calling wherewith we were called, that excludes a spirit of arrogance or brutality which is demeaning towards other people.

What should be more natural for a Christian than to practise humility? The apostle's teaching in this book from the very beginning of the text includes an overarching emphasis on the graciousness of our redemption. If my entrance into the church and into God's kingdom is not based on my merit, but strictly and simply on the grace of God and his election, then I have everything to be humble about. As Paul says elsewhere, 'Let him who boasts boast in the Lord' (1 Corinthians 1:31; 2 Corinthians 10:17). It is fitting, then, that the response to the call of God be one rooted and grounded in humility and gentleness.

Paul adds in verse 2, **be patient**. The word here in the Greek, is *macrothumia*, that is long-suffering. The opposite of long suffering is a person with a hair trigger temper, who explodes in fury, rage and rejection at the slightest provocation. A counsellor once made this analogy: every human being has, in his personality, certain minefields, made up of mines that are hidden beneath the surface. These are sensitive points where we respond out of proportion to the situation because these are areas wherein we are easily provoked. In some people's field, there may be only one or two mines for every ten acres of field. These people are rather easy to get along with. With other people, there is no safe passageway through their field, because it is wall-to-wall mines. They are touchy, sensitive, always getting angry, always getting upset, and always causing problems.

If you get a group of ten people together for any enterprise, whether it is a church function or a job at work, it only takes one person who is a walking wall-to-wall minefield to destroy the morale of everyone else in the group. What happens in marriages when people are exploding in anger at simple provocations again and again?

It is impossible for any two people to live together without having some point of conflict. We all find places and things that irritate or annoy us, where we disagree among ourselves. The question is, how we learn to live with other people.

To be worthy of the calling of Christ we must reflect the character of God. God is not without wrath, but he is slow to anger, and he doesn't hold grudges. God doesn't let his anger develop into bitterness. As his people, we are to reflect the same spirit of patience that we ask God to display towards us. Isn't this behind the request in the Lord's Prayer: Forgive us our debts as we forgive our debtors. A forgiving and charitable spirit is characteristic of the Christian life, not one that is argumentative, provocative, or explosive.

Every church, every congregation, will have members who are simply not charitable in their judgments of other people, and who are not patient and long-suffering. They will be the opposite. They will be abrasive, combative, rude and insensitive. Those are the works of the flesh.

One dangerous thing within the body of Christ is that long-suffering may be confused with indifference. Churches which adopt a liberal theology tend to be very tolerant of just about any form of behaviour or theology. But when you get into a conservative Christian community, where people hold the truths of Scripture to be precious, you will often find people ready to fight over every minor point of dispute in theology.

There are limits to this long-suffering, as Paul pointed out to the Corinthian congregation when he insisted that the incestuous man be disciplined (1 Corinthians 5:1-5). But the purpose of the discipline was to lead the man to repentance. When he did subsequently repent, the church at Corinth took the opposite position and they were now so strong and severe in their judgment on this man that they would not allow him to be restored to the fellowship of the church. Paul had to write again, telling them to welcome him back and restore him to the full fellowship of the church (2 Corinthians 2:6-11). Hence, we find, in the pristine Christian community at Corinth, under the direct tutelage of the apostle Paul, imbalance in this direction. First they are too long-suffering, then they are not long-suffering enough.

We can sum up the matter in this way: the Scriptures tell

us that we are not to be so long-suffering that we never rebuke, admonish or exhort. At the same time, however, the characteristic spirit of one who is being led by the Spirit of God is to be non-judgmental. The spirit that is to be manifested in long-suffering is the spirit of love: love for God and love for people: **bearing with one another in love.**

Notice in verse 3 that they should be making **every effort to keep the unity of the Spirit through the bond of peace.** The Holy Spirit is not a cause of contentiousness, for he binds people together in peace, not only in terms of cessation from military conflict, but in terms of personal relationships. This is vital for the health of the body of Christ, as it is for any community. Here the Spirit is called the 'bond' of that peace. He is literally the cement that binds people together.

Then in verse 4 is this great statement describing the basis of Christian unity: **There is one body and one Spirit – just as you were called to one hope when you were called – one Lord, one faith, one baptism; one God and Father of all, who is over all and through all and in all.**

Notice, there are several things that Paul expounds here as points that unify the Christian community.

There is *one body of Christ.* There may be many denominations, but there is a distinction in theology between the visible church and the invisible church. The visible church may be distressingly and sorely fractured and fragmented into all different kinds of denominations and groups, but the invisible church is the true body of Christ. Everyone who is in Christ, and in whom Christ dwells, is a member of this one universal church.

There is *one Spirit* who links us to Christ, who dwells within us and who joins us together as a body. It is in the fellowship of the Holy Spirit that the unity of the body of Christ is guaranteed.

There is the same ultimate goal: the consummation of the

kingdom of God. We may argue over the specifics of that consummation and when it is going to come, whether it will be pre, post or a-millennial. But ultimately there is only *one hope*: the triumph of Jesus, as the King of kings and Lord of lords.

There is only *one Lord* of the church. We don't have a church that is ruled by a heavenly committee. Jesus Christ is Lord.

There is only *one Christian faith*. There may be many manifestations of that faith, many debates about the content of that faith, but ultimately there is only one apostolic faith which has been delivered once and for all.

There is only *one baptism*, one initiatory rite into the visible church of Jesus Christ. Even though the church of Christ is divided into different denominations, nearly every Christian community embraces some form of baptism as a sign of one's membership in the visible body of Christ.

The ultimate unity is found in the character of God himself: *one God and Father of all*. We speak abstractly, perhaps loosely, about God as the Supreme Being. But if ever those words meant anything, they certainly capture what is stated in verse 6: **one God and Father of all, who is over all and through all and in all**. This is absolute supremacy. God is over everything. He permeates all things. He is in all things.

All of these characteristics spell out for us the basis of unity in the body of Christ.

The church in the first century was threatened by a division between Jewish believers and Gentile believers. Paul demonstrates that God is bringing people from different backgrounds, nations and languages and is moulding them into one body, the universal church of Jesus Christ.

Diversity of gifts

In verse 7, the tone changes as Paul moves away from unity to diversity. One of the beautiful things about the New Testament church is that it is a community. But the New Testament does not advocate uniformity, where everybody has to look alike, speak alike, and do alike. No, the body of Christ is a beautiful mixture of unity and diversity. In that sense it is a microcosm of the universe itself.

But to each one of us grace has been given as Christ apportioned it. Every person who is in Christ is a *charismatic*. When we use the term 'charismatic' today, we are describing somebody who has some special endowment or gift. The word 'charismatic' comes from the Greek word, *charis*, which means gift, or grace. The apostle states that all Christians have been gifted by the grace of God. But they don't get the same gifts. Therein lies the beautiful diversity of this organism that is called 'the church'. Paul elaborates this theme in 1 Corinthian 12, when he talks about the eye, the nose, the ear, and so on, with his analogy of the human body.

> **This is why it says: 'When he ascended on high, he led captives in his train and gave gifts to men.' (What does 'he ascended' mean except that he also descended to the lower, earthly regions? He who descended is the very one who ascended higher than all the heavens, in order to fill the whole universe)** (verses 8-10).

When Paul says in verse 9 that Christ 'descended to the lower earthly regions', he is not referring to Christ's death and burial but to his incarnation, when he became a man and lived on earth. It is the fact that he descended before he ascended that makes his ascension unique from other ascensions.

In the Old Testament the idea of ascending was linked to two activities. First, it described drawing near to the presence of God. The Tabernacle was set on a hill and people went up to it. Later, the Temple was built on a mountain in Jerusalem and there is a section in the Book of Psalms, called the Psalms of Ascent (120-134), which describe the worshippers' approach to the Temple at the festival periods of Israel. So Jesus, when he ascended, entered God's presence.

Secondly, 'ascending' was connected to the enthronement after victory, when the spoils of battle would be brought up to God's house and captives from the battle would be led through the city. This reference to captives is not a description of Satan but to Christ's people whom Christ defeated in the sense of destroying their sins and setting them free. He presented the train, comprising his people, to the Father.

After Jesus ascended into heaven in triumph and sat at the right hand of God, perhaps the first act of the new King was Pentecost (Acts 2), when he poured out his Holy Spirit to gift every member of his church. As we noted earlier, God has given a gift to each Christian. However, in verse 11, Paul mentions gifts of leadership in the church: **It was he who gave some to be apostles, some to be prophets, some to be evangelists, and some to be pastors and teachers.**

Apostles, as I discuss elsewhere in my comments on 2:20 and 3:2, were those individuals chosen by Christ to be the foundation stones of the church and as such ceased to exist when the original apostles died. *Prophets* (again see comments on 2:20 and 3:2) were closely linked with the apostles and, among other activities, helped write the New Testament. Since the Bible is complete, there are not any prophets today. *Evangelists* are taken by some to be assistants to the apostles and so no longer exist. But the term could describe 'church planters' who develop new churches. The fourth type of leader is the person who is *both a pastor and a teacher* (Paul links both terms together in the one individual).

In verse 12 we are given the explicit reason why these

offices are given to the church: **To prepare God's people for works of service, so that the body of Christ may be built up**. This passage speaks boldly to the twentieth century church. Somehow, somewhere, an idea emerged and became very popular in the Christian community; so popular in fact, that it has now become almost an iron-clad tradition. It is that the ministry of the church is to be done by the paid, professional, theologically-trained clergy. According to this view, the whole purpose of the laity is to receive the benefits of ministry, in terms of preaching, counselling, comfort, and those other things that we seek to provide in the church. But the reason why certain gifts are given for leadership is to equip the believers for ministry. The church is to be a mobilised army.

I remember an old Methodist minister once asked me this question: 'Do you think the church has been called by Christ to be an army or a hospital?' I was a bit impatient when he asked the question and I said, 'There is no doubt in my mind: the church has been established by Christ to be an army, not to be a hospital.' But he explained to me that it is not an either/or situation. Armies, in order to be effective, must be very sensitive in caring for their wounded. What that minister was trying to tell me was that, though I was all excited about reaching a lost world with missionary outreach and the evangelism of the church, there is always a major work to be done within the church in terms of ministering to the needs of the people. And certainly he was right about that.

But in addition to ministering to the needs of people, leaders are called to train people, to give them the equipment, the tools, the knowledge and the skills necessary for works of service. The most effective churches that I know are churches where the ministerial staff devote many hours in training and mobilising their congregations to be mighty armies of saints, as they minister to a dying world.

So that the body of Christ may be built up. The gifts are given to leaders, not to tear apart the body of Christ, but for the edification, the uplifting, the strengthening and the building up of the people **until we all reach unity in the faith and in the knowledge of the Son of God and become mature, attaining to the whole measure of the fulness of Christ** (verses 12-13).

Eric Alexander remarks on this passage that the principle of unity is inviolable, having been established by God. The practice of unity, however, is violable, being broken all the time. The goal of maturity in Christ is to successfully unite those two. How ironic it is that the very unity of the faith, and unity of the knowledge of God, is in fact the very thing that causes schisms. Paul here is speaking doctrinally–there is but one true gospel to which all believers should adhere. How desperately sad is the fact that the church is known by schism, not unity; ignorance, not knowledge; and indecisiveness rather than maturity. How it must break God's heart to see us continue in such a poverty stricken condition in light of what he has done, stands ready to do, has the resources to accomplish, and has defined as our calling in Christ.

Importance of development

Verse 14 says, **Then we will no longer be infants, tossed back and forth by the waves, and blown here and there by every wind of teaching and by the cunning and craftiness of men in their deceitful scheming**. One of the greatest obstacles encountered in a teaching ministry is this idea, pervasive in the Christian church, that there is no benefit to be had by the laity in serious study of the Word of God or in the study of theology. We have elevated to the level of an ideal the idea of having a simple, childlike faith.

We find people saying, 'I want my faith to be simple and

childlike, I don't need to know any theology. All I need to know is Jesus.' That sentiment is a childish sentiment and, I suggest to you, it is a sinful sentiment.

The Bible calls us to be like children in two specific ways: first, Jesus says that unless we approach the kingdom of God as little children, we will never enter it (Matthew 18:3). That is, we are to approach the kingdom of God with a simple, childlike trust in God. The second way in which the Scripture directs us to be children is, 'In regard to evil be infants, but in your thinking be adults' (1 Corinthians 14:20). That text contrasts the point at which we are to be adult and the point at which we are to be infantile. We are to be infant-like in respect of evil. Babies sin, but their sins are not as sophisticated as some of the complex and intricate sins of adults. Babies are by no means innocent, but they are relatively innocent compared to the machinations of the mature. So in that regard, we are called to be infants in evil, but in our thinking to be adults.

There is a close connection between simplicity and naivety. Believers who have not been deeply trained and matured in the things of God are vulnerable and exposed to every wind of doctrine that blows through the church. When I was a child a new thing came on the market. It was a beany with a propeller on the top. I bought the beany with the propeller on the top. And then shortly after that, the hula-hoop came out, and I bought the hula-hoop. Then yo-yos were in vogue, after that, water pistols were the rage. All of these things were short-lived. As children we were caught up in these fads and you were out of it if you didn't have a beany with a propeller on the top, or a hula-hoop. As adults, we are not supposed to be so susceptible to every fad that comes down the line, but often we are. We are almost captivated by the latest trends in style and so on, and the last thing that we want to be is out of it, and not up with the latest fashion and the latest trend.

We see this in the world of theology. In theological scholarship, in many cases, you are looked down upon if you are not committed to the latest radical departure from classical orthodox Christianity. Have you ever stopped to think how unlikely it is, after two thousand years of intense examination and reflection, that any substantively new understanding of the Christian faith would be discovered now? We find new discoveries in astronomy, new discoveries in medical science and so on. But here we are looking at the same source, the same material that has been sifted over and over again for two thousand years. There is something stable about the classical understanding of the Christian faith.

Certainly, there will be new insights, new understandings and applications of the word of God. But I get far more out of reading Martin Luther's understanding of the New Testament than I do from contemporary scholars, who are so caught up with the latest fad in theology.

Even in evangelical Christianity there are certain winds of doctrine that become popular and sweep through the church. Usually they are an influence from outside the church. For example, today we are seeing this unbelievable impact of an alleged new type of metaphysical philosophy called New Age thinking. There is nothing new about New Age thinking. The New Age movement has its roots in first century gnosticism, and even before that, in various forms of Eastern philosophy which claim that we are one with God and are able to exercise a control over our environment by positive thinking and that sort of thing. As ghastly as those concepts are, in relation to the Christian faith, we see them making inroads into evangelical Christianity. It is a new wind of doctrine to borrow from New Age thinking ideas that are utterly incompatible with New Testament Christianity. We are exposed to these things and vulnerable to them because we simply do not have a mature understanding of the truth of God.

For every sin in the world, there is somebody who has tried to write a moral justification for it. Today, scholars eloquently defend abortion. There were theologians in Germany and in Russia who eloquently tried to justify the actions taken by Hitler and Stalin. But the means used are deceit, craftiness, and scheming. How are we going to see through that? Have a mature understanding of the word of God and you won't be taken in by crafty and deceitful speech.

Instead, speaking the truth in love (verse 15). It is the task of Christians to be people of the truth. They are called to search the truth, to understand the truth, to communicate the truth. But it is not simply abstract propositional utterance that they are to make. They are to hold this truth that is precious to them *in love.*

Of course, this phrase, 'speaking the truth in love', is used for all kinds of devious personal attacks that one believer will make on another. We have heard it said many times, 'Brother, I want to speak the truth in love to you.' It is important that when we are engaged in admonition or exhortation or confrontation with a brother who is overcome in sin, we call attention to the truth in an extraordinarily compassionate and tender and loving spirit. Unfortunately, the people who most often preface comments by saying, 'Brother, I want to speak the truth in love,' are the ones who are the most insensitive and the most injurious in violating other people by acid and destructive criticism. But when we speak the truth in love, **we will in all things grow up into him who is the Head, that is, Christ** (verse 15). To grow up into Christ, no longer to be children or adolescents in our faith but to grow up into all aspects of Christ, that is the goal.

From him the whole body, joined and held together by every supporting ligament, grows and builds itself up in love, as each part does its work (verse 16). Paul uses his frequent image of the physical organism, where each part must make its contribution in harmony with the others. All of the parts are vital and essential for the healthy and complete functioning of the body. So every member in the body of Christ is gifted by the Holy Spirit, and is called by the Holy Spirit to participate in the ministry of Christ. Every person in the body of Christ has a significant task to perform. No-one is insignificant; no-one is unimportant. There is no such thing as a misfit in the body of Christ because Christ himself, the head of the body, is the one who makes sure that we fit together and knit together into the unity of his body.

8
Christian Living
(4:17–5:20)

So I tell you this, and insist on it in the Lord, that you must no longer live as the Gentiles do, in the futility of their thinking. They are darkened in their understanding and separated from the life of God because of the ignorance that is in them due to the hardening of their hearts. Having lost all sensitivity, they have given themselves over to sensuality so as to indulge in every kind of impurity, with a continual lust for more.

You, however, did not come to know Christ that way. Surely you heard of him and were taught in him in accordance with the truth that is in Jesus. You were taught, with regard to your former way of life, to put off your old self, which is being corrupted by its deceitful desires; to be made new in the attitude of your minds; and to put on the new self, created to be like God in true righteousness and holiness.

Therefore each of you must put off falsehood and speak truthfully to his neighbour, for we are all members of one body. "In your anger do not sin": Do not let the sun go down while you are still angry, and do not give the devil a foothold. He who has been stealing must steal no longer, but must work, doing something useful with his own hands, that he may have something to share with those in need.

Do not let any unwholesome talk come out of your mouths, but only what is helpful for building others up according to their needs, that it may benefit those who listen. And do not grieve the Holy Spirit of God, with whom you were sealed for the day of redemption. Get rid of all bitterness, rage and anger, brawling and slander, along with every form of malice. Be kind and compassionate to one another, forgiving each other, just as in Christ God forgave you.

Be imitators of God, therefore, as dearly loved children

and live a life of love, just as Christ loved us and gave himself up for us as a fragrant offering and sacrifice to God.

But among you there must not be even a hint of sexual immorality, or of any kind of impurity, or of greed, because these are improper for God's holy people. Nor should there be obscenity, foolish talk or coarse joking, which are out of place, but rather thanksgiving. For of this you can be sure: No immoral, impure or greedy person — such a man is an idolater — has any inheritance in the kingdom of Christ and of God. Let no-one deceive you with empty words, for because of such things God's wrath comes on those who are disobedient. Therefore do not be partners with them.

For you were once darkness, but now you are light in the Lord. Live as children of light (for the fruit of the light consists in all goodness, righteousness and truth) and find out what pleases the Lord. Have nothing to do with the fruitless deeds of darkness, but rather expose them. For it is shameful even to mention what the disobedient do in secret. But everything exposed by the light becomes visible, for it is light that makes everything visible. This is why it is said: "Wake up, O sleeper, rise from the dead, and Christ will shine on you."

Be very careful, then, how you live — not as unwise but as wise, making the most of every opportunity, because the days are evil. Therefore do not be foolish, but understand what the Lord's will is. Do not get drunk on wine, which leads to debauchery. Instead, be filled with the Spirit. Speak to one another with psalms, hymns and spiritual songs. Sing and make music in your heart to the Lord, always giving thanks to God the Father for everything, in the name of our Lord Jesus Christ.

In verse 17, Paul shifts from this theology of the unity and diversity of the mystical body of Christ to spell out behavioural patterns that he expects to see in the church and in the lives of the saints. Often in Paul's letters he moves from very weighty doctrinal teaching, sometimes abruptly, to the practical, ethical, behavioural applications of that truth. Here he says: **So I tell you this, and insist on it in the Lord, that you must no longer live as the Gentiles do, in the futility of their thinking. They are darkened in their understanding and separated from the life of God because of the ignorance that is in them due to the hardening of their hearts** (verses 17,18).

Having really attained a mature understanding of the things of God, then, a believer is not going to live like the Gentiles, who are ignorant of the things of God and who don't have God in their thinking. Their thinking is not informed by divine revelation and they don't have the perspective of eternity that is given to Christians in the word of God. The pagan mind is never theocentric (God-centred); the Christian mind must be theocentric. God must be at the centre, informing the understanding and shaping opinions about everything.

Paul further describes the pagans as **having lost all sensitivity, they have given themselves over to sensuality so as to indulge in every kind of impurity, with a continual lust for more** (verse 19). Notice that since they do not have God in their minds, then they do not have God in their actions. Because of the darkness of their minds and the hardness of their hearts, they have given themselves to a sensual lifestyle that rests on impurity and greed.

Paul reminds the saints in Ephesus: **You, however, did not come to know Christ that way** (verse 20). One of the most demoralising things for those seeking to live a virtuous life according to the Christian ethic, is to be in an environment or a community or a society that is in a completely different value-system structure. We are all vulnerable to the 'everybody is doing it' mentality. We tend to take our norms for behaviour from what is going on around us, or from what is legal in secular society.

If society says it is legal for a woman to have an abortion on demand, then some Christians go ahead and have abortions on demand, forgetting that in the final analysis it doesn't matter what everybody else is doing and it doesn't matter what the state says is legal or illegal. We are to march to a different drumbeat, for we are to live according to the commandments of Christ.

Paul reminds these Gentile converts of what they had been taught:

Surely you heard of him and were taught in him in accordance with the truth that is in Jesus. You were taught, with regard to your former way of life, to put off your old self, which is being corrupted by its deceitful desires; to be made new in the attitude of your minds; and to put on the new self, created to be like God in true righteousness and holiness (verses 21-24).

We seem to be moral schizoids. It is a struggle between what the Bible calls the 'old man' and the 'new man'. Once I have been made alive to God through his divine initiative, quickened by his regenerating grace, my heart now throbs with spiritual life. There is now a radical discontinuity between my new self and my old self. It is not, however, a *total* discontinuity. A link remains between the old man and the new man. The old man has been dealt a death blow; his destination is certain, but he is not yet dead. As Christians we are to mortify the flesh by destroying the old nature. We are to feed the new man with all the means of grace that God has appointed and at the same time starve the old man by denying him the occasions for sin. It is the indwelling power of the Holy Spirit who works this renewal from within as we struggle in this spiritual warfare.

It is important to understand that truth is absolutely vital and essential to new life. It is truth that changes our behaviour; a sober, clear understanding of God's truth is what changes lives.

Paul is saying: if you are of the truth, if you have learned the truth, if you see the sanctity of the truth, then speak truth. We are not called to be deceivers or liars. God is a God of truth, and his people are called to have an enormously high standard of truth. **Therefore each of you must put off falsehood and speak truthfully to his neighbour, for we are all members of one body** (verse 25).

Now verses 26 and 27 give some very strange advice: **"In your anger do not sin": Do not let the sun go down while you are still angry, and do not give the devil a foothold**. Notice that the apostle does not say, 'Never be angry.' In fact, the imperative form is in the positive: 'In your anger, do not sin.'

The Bible has much to say about anger. We have a tendency to think that anger, in and of itself, is a sin. We imagine that there is something intrinsically wrong about getting angry. If this was the case, however, it would reflect badly on the character of God. You see, the Bible speaks frequently about the wrath of God and there are episodes in the Gospel narrative of the life of Jesus, where he manifested anger (e.g. Mark 3:5).

Christian anger

We tend to use a euphemism for such displays of anger as 'righteous indignation', and it is a very meaningful concept. There is such a thing as justifiable indignation. God is perfectly justified in being provoked to anger by our sinfulness. So we have to understand that anger, in and of itself, is not evil. But anger can very easily become an occasion for evil, an open door to Satanic enticements and temptation. This is simply because anger can be a very strong emotion and we can lose control of ourselves in what we call the 'heat' of anger.

The virtue of self-control is listed frequently in the New Testament as an attribute we should show in the Christian life. If, in our anger, we lose control of ourselves then, of course, we are no longer manifesting the virtue of self-control. Anger can give way to violence, violence to brutality, brutality to war. Anger can also become malicious and can change into resentment or the holding of a grudge. So Paul gives the practical advice: **Do not let the sun go down while you are still angry**. What does that figurative expression indicate? To have the sun go down while you are still angry means that you take it to bed with you and the situation is not resolved. The anger is kept inside and it begins to boil and seethe, perhaps turning into bitterness. The author of Hebrews writes that bitterness is an attitude of the heart, by which people can have their whole personalities spoiled or defiled (12:15). We have all met people who manifest a spirit of bitterness, or a spirit of hostility. They seem to be at war with the world. They walk around life with a chip on their shoulder. They get cynical. They get sour in their interpersonal dealings with people. All of these things can be the result of unresolved anger.

The emotional life is to be under the sovereignty of God, and ruled by the Holy Spirit of God. We are capable of all different kinds of emotion, including joy, sorrow and bitterness. Some of these emotions are perfectly legitimate, others are not.

For example, grief is a legitimate emotion. Jesus was a

man of sorrows, acquainted with grief (Isaiah 53:3). In fact, there are times when the Bible commends us for displaying the emotion of grief: Blessed are those who mourn (Matthew 5:4). But there is a fine line between grief and self-pity, between grief and bitterness.

It is important to labour this point because sometimes we have the feeling that any display of anger is sinful, and therefore we have a sub-cultural taboo against the expression of anger. That can cause people to deceive themselves and to have no ventilation for anger which, when we hold it in, tends to mount up like a pressure tank waiting to explode. Then when the explosion comes, it is out of control, violent and destructive.

Practically speaking, one of the best ways to express anger to another person is simply to say, 'I am angry about this.' There is nothing violent or destructive about a simple statement like that. Of course, the question as to whether that anger is just or unjust remains, and that has to be examined in every particular circumstance.

There is another dimension of anger that ought to be mentioned, namely, the tremendous impact anger has on our interpersonal relationships. My practical rule-of-thumb is this: whenever we see anger being manifested we need to look behind the anger to its source. In my judgment, one hundred times out of one hundred, this is some kind of pain. One of the most important questions we can ask someone who is manifesting hostility, cynicism or bitterness is the simple question (phrased as a question and not as an accusation): Why are you angry?

I once read a report about some clinical psychologists who said that in communication between two people, the message that is transmitted works out like this. About 10% is dependent on the words that are spoken, 35% on the tone of voice, and 55% on the body language, gestures or facial expression – the non-verbal dimensions that accompany our speech. So if I say gently to somebody, 'Why are you angry?' that's one way of asking the question. Or I can say to that person, with a stern look on my face, 'Why are you angry?' When I say it like that I am not only asking a question, I am making an accusation, and probably contributing to the escalation of the anger. If we can find out why a person is angry we can generally get to its root cause, which, as I said, one hundred times out of one hundred, will be some kind of pain.

Think for a moment how you respond to these two comments. Somebody comes up to you and says, 'I am angry!' How do you respond to that? Another person comes up to you and says, 'I am really hurting!' How do you respond to that? Are your responses the same? I doubt it. Mine certainly wouldn't be the same. I would respond differently to a person who says, 'I'm hurting!' because it strikes a chord in my soul and provokes a spirit of compassion. I want to hear why that person is hurting, to know if there is anything I can do to help them. Yet if a person comes up to me and says, 'I'm angry!', then I'm thinking defensively. Are they mad at me? Why should they be mad at me? Well, I'll get mad at them! Then we get into this battle that is so destructive.

What I am trying to get across here is that, in most cases, when a person says, 'I'm angry!' what he is really saying is, 'I'm hurting!' A tremendous link exists between anger and pain. Why do I say this?

There are various things that make people angry, for example, physical pain. If somebody comes up and slaps you across the face, chances are you will get angry because anger is a response to the physical pain.

But there are other kinds of pain that make us angry. One of the most frequent causes of anger is frustration, and/or disappointment. Think how closely related frustration and disappointment are. If I set my hopes on something and it fails to come to pass, that frustrates me, causes pain, and I will get angry.

We distinguish various types of anger, including what is called 'misdirected' anger. Have you ever heard this expression: 'You are just taking it out on me'? We do take our frustrations and our disappointments out on innocent people. The wife is at home during the day, and the kids have been giving her all kinds of trouble. Also, the dog tears up the curtains, the toaster breaks, and the car won't start. Then the husband comes home from work and the wife bites his head off when he walks through the door. He says, 'Wait, wait a minute, I wasn't even here!'

Another kind of anger that we encounter is what I call 'situational' anger. It is very closely related, because it is a kind of misdirected anger. It arises in frustrating situations over which no-one has any control. You have been planning for weeks to have a picnic and you have bought all the provisions, even rented a pavilion in the park. You pack up the kids and set off but when you get there a cloudburst comes and it starts to rain. All of your plans are destroyed by something beyond anybody's control, by the storm, by the situation. But you are frustrated, you are disappointed, you are hurt; and that can produce an anger that is destructive towards those around you.

Stealing

There is more practical advice in verse 28: **He who has been stealing must steal no longer.** There is no room for theft in the kingdom of God. One of the ten commandments protects the rights of private property: 'You shall not steal' (Exodus 20:15). Stealing is when I wilfully and consciously take for myself somebody else's property.

God abominates stealing. It is interesting to me that two of the ten commandments thoroughly respect the rights of private property: You shall not steal, and, You shall not covet (Exodus 20:15, 17). God says that not only is it wrong to steal, it is wrong to desire what is not yours, and want for your own what belongs to somebody else.

Sanctity of labour

The Bible not only has strong teaching about the sanctity of life, it also has strong demands about the sanctity of labour. We are not allowed to get our worldly needs fulfilled by theft. Rather, we are called upon by God to labour for our possessions: **but must work, doing something useful with his own hands, that he may have something to share with those in need** (verse 28).

Use of the tongue

The Bible often speaks about how much damage we can do to other people with our tongues. **Do not let any unwholesome talk come out of your mouths, but only what is helpful for building others up according to their needs, that it may benefit those who listen** (verse 29). Indeed, the Holy Spirit can be grieved by our wrong speaking: **And do not grieve the Holy Spirit of God, with whom you were sealed for the day of redemption** (verse 30). The Holy Spirit's work is to sanctify us. When we resort to stealing, cursing, and bitterness, we are not only resisting the Holy Spirit, we are grieving him.

Get rid of all bitterness, rage and anger, brawling and slander, along with every form of malice (verse 31). These represent the fall-out vices which flow from anger that is out of control. The opposite is intended: **Be kind and compassionate to one another, forgiving each other just as in Christ God forgave you**. One of the most terrifying elements of the Lord's Prayer is the petition, 'Forgive us our debts, as we forgive our debtors' (Matthew 6:12). We tend to be far more ungenerous in forgiving others than God is in forgiving us. If God were to be as reluctant to forgive as we are in forgiving those who sin against us, we would be in serious trouble. As Christians we are forgiven people. We are likewise called to be forgiving people. Jesus clearly sets forth an ethic of charity in his teaching and in his behaviour with those who wrong us. An unwillingness to forgive clearly has no place in the kingdom, and may in fact signal that such a one has not experienced the initial forgiveness of God in his or her life.

These verses serve as a bridge to chapter 5, where we get a full expression of what it means to imitate God and to live the life that is governed by love.

Imitators of God

In this fifth chapter we have a magnificent expression of what it means to live a life of godliness. And it begins in verse 1 with a very important admonition: **Be imitators of God, therefore, as dearly loved children**. One of the all-time best selling books ever produced in the history of the Christian church, written by St Thomas a Kempis, was entitled, *The Imitation of Christ*.

In the New Testament Christ is described as the express image of God (2 Corinthians 4:4; Colossians 1:15). He is the brightness of the glory of God (Hebrews 1:3). In the person of Jesus and in the life that he lived, we see what our humanity is to be like. Again, we go back to creation and we see that man is made in the image and in the likeness of God (Genesis 1:26, 27), not in the sense that God has a body, but in terms of our nature. We are called to be living images that reflect and communicate the character of God himself. Elsewhere

God commands this of his people: 'Be holy, because I am holy' (Leviticus 11:44-45; 19:2; 20:7; 1 Peter 1:16). That is, our lives are to imitate, to copy, the character of God.

An imitation is a copy based upon an authentic original. The authentic fountainhead, the original source of righteousness is God himself, and God's people are called to bear witness to the original and to the authentic.

It is interesting that Paul conjoins the idea of imitation with the link that we have to God as his children. Remember that the apostle, in this letter, has spelled out in detail the glorious inheritance that is the Christian's, of having been adopted into the family of God. As the sons and daughters of God, we are to reflect the character of our parent, our heavenly Father.

And then he says, in verse 2, **and live a life of love, just as Christ loved us and gave himself up for us as a fragrant offering and sacrifice to God**. Paul is expanding upon how we are to imitate God. The way that imitation is to be expressed is by following the earthly example of Christ. Jesus' love was a love that manifested itself in self-sacrifice. He offered himself for others. His offering and sacrifice fulfilled all of the ritual sacrifices of the Old Testament. The sweetest fragrance, the most beautiful aroma that God has ever detected emanating from this planet, was the aroma of the perfect sacrifice of Jesus that was offered once and for all on the cross. As Christ imitated the Father, so we are called to imitate him. We do that when we live a life of love.

In our own generation, we have witnessed the advancement in both the secular culture and the Christian church of what has been called 'the New Morality'. Joseph Fletcher's book called *Situation Ethics* became a best-seller in the 1960s, and it was linked, at points, with the emergence of the so-called New Morality. The 'situational ethics' thesis was this: the Christian faith is not based chiefly on a list of rules, commandments, and laws. There is only one moral imperative, only one overarching law, to be found in the Christian life. It is the law of love: to love God and do what love requires in any given situation.

Fletcher appealed to Pauline statements such as, 'love is the fulfilment of the law' (Romans 13:10). The famous quotation of Augustine, 'Love God and do as you please', was twisted beyond any recognition from its original intent. Augustine meant that if our hearts are motivated internally by the proper spirit of love for God, then we will be able to do as we please because love for God will constrain us to do only those things that please the Lord. That is, the supreme motivation for obeying the law of God both in its letter and its spirit, is a genuine affection for the Father. But Augustine never had in mind the idea that if you have some feeling of affection for God in your heart, then you can go ahead and disregard the commandments of God.

Of course, Fletcher doesn't say it that crassly either. But he does allow that there may be situations where, for example, if the overarching consideration is love, extra-marital sexual relationships may be quite acceptable in the sight of God. There are various studies on human sexuality produced by commissions and committees of mainline denominations which have set forth the possibility that within the context of love, it may be all right to be engaged in extra-marital sexual relationships, premarital sexual involvement, and even homosexual relationships. The idea, at the bottom line, is this: if you love, then your behaviour can be determined, circumscribed and justified by that love.

But among you there must not be even a hint of sexual immorality, or of any kind of impurity, or of greed, because these are improper for God's holy people (verse 3). Here we see the sharp contrast between Paul's understanding of what it means to live a life of love, and the contemporary cultural understanding of what it means. In Paul's mind nothing could be further from a life of love than to be involved in sexual relationships that are forbidden by God.

Paul doesn't say, 'Love God and do as you please.' But he says, 'If you want to know what love demands, then pay attention to what the prime source of love requires. God's law reveals to us what is pleasing to him.' The point of this passage is that, if we are his children and we want to imitate him, we must seek to obey his laws. This is not to be done slavishly, out of servile fear or out of some rigid, stoical desire for rule-keeping, but rather from a profound desire to express our love for the Father.

Paul, as he did in chapter 4, comes back to the importance of the speech of the Christian: **Nor should there be obscenity, foolish talk or coarse joking, which are out of place, but rather thanksgiving** (verse 4). Elsewhere he commends a kind of speech that is 'seasoned with salt' (Colossians 4:6). Paul is not against the use of witticisms; nor is he against the person who has a fine command and articulation with regard to language. In fact the Scripture has many, many things to say about the beauty inherent in the very function of speech. It is not by accident that God Incarnate is called the 'Word' of God, and his apostles were called ministers of the Word.

Words are important. Jesus said that it is not what goes into a man's mouth that defiles a man, it is what comes out of his mouth (Matthew 15:11). The Scriptures often come back and warn us to guard our tongues. James gives a whole chapter to it in his letter.

Paul speaks about a misuse of language; not about joking, but coarse joking. Filthy language and rude forms of speech are not appropriate to the lifestyle of the Christian, for our speech should be appropriate to our relationship with God. Our mouths should be organs of thanksgiving.

For of this you can be sure: No immoral, impure or greedy person – such a man is an idolater – has any inheritance in the kingdom of Christ and of God (verse 5). This statement may frighten you, for it may seem to be in striking contradiction to everything else that the Bible teaches us about salvation. Paul suggests that anyone who covets and anyone who is guilty of immorality or impurity, has forfeited once and for all an inheritance in the kingdom of Christ and of God. But this statement is elliptical, that is, this statement leaves things unstated that are clearly understood. Paul is not saying here that if you were ever guilty of coveting somebody else's possessions that thereby you are eternally disqualified from the kingdom of God.

He is talking about a style of life that is characteristic. That is, if the basic characteristic of your life is sexual immorality, impurity or covetousness, then as long as you remain in that state, you remain out of the kingdom of God. One may make a profession of faith in Christ, and then continue in a licentious lifestyle. This would reveal quicker than anything else that the profession of faith is false and the person is not in the kingdom of God.

Verse 6 anticipates that it is possible for people to think that they are safely in the kingdom of God because they have been given false assurances by those with glib tongues and smooth talking promises. **Let no one deceive you with empty words, for because of such things God's wrath comes on those who are disobedient**. This passage is a diatribe against any type of Antinomianism that says there is no abiding law we are required to keep.

There is a pernicious doctrine in the evangelical church in our day which says that all a person has to do to be redeemed is to accept Jesus as Saviour; he doesn't have to receive him as Lord. This dichotomy between Saviour and Lord is the clearest, most blatant form of Antinomianism seen in the twentieth century. The moment we are regenerated, the Spirit of God comes to dwell in our hearts to motivate us, to give us an obedient heart. Now we love the law of God, not because it is the means by which we are redeemed, but because it reveals to us what pleases our Father whom we love. The moment we embrace Jesus as Saviour, we bow to him as Lord, and seek to show our love for him by obeying his commandments.

So if anyone comes and tells you that as a Christian you don't have to be concerned about keeping commandments or obeying the law of God, you are listening to someone who is speaking empty words, words that could deceive you. And Paul says, 'Don't let that happen, don't let anyone deceive you with empty words, for because of this very type of thing, the wrath of God comes upon those who are disobedient.' In the Sermon on the Mount, Jesus said that many will come to him on the last day saying, 'Lord, Lord, didn't we do this in your name, didn't we do that in your name?' And he will say, 'I never knew you. Away from me, you evildoers!' (Matthew 7:23).

Therefore do not be partners with them (verse 7). I take this to mean, don't get involved, or participate in any form of the spirit of Antinomianism. **For you were once darkness, but now you are light in the Lord. Live as children of light (for the fruit of the light consists in all goodness, righteousness and truth) and find out what pleases the Lord** (verses 8-10). Goodness, righteousness, and truth are the marks and the fruit of being children of the light. If you want to know what it means to be children of the light, then you must try to learn what is pleasing to the Lord. There is no way of learning more accurately or more quickly about what is pleasing to God, than studying the law of God. It reveals to us what things God takes delight in and what things God hates.

So Paul says: **Have nothing to do with the fruitless deeds of darkness, but rather expose them. For it is shameful even to mention what the disobedient do in secret. But everything exposed by the light becomes visible, for it is light that makes everything visible. This is why it is said: 'Wake up, O sleeper, rise from the dead, and Christ will shine on you'** (verses 11-14). As people of light, we have participated in a spiritual resurrection. Therefore, our lives cannot be lived as men and women who look for the darkness to do those things that we would be ashamed to do in public. Rather, we are to reflect Jesus' injunction: 'Let your light shine before men, that they may see your good deeds and praise your Father in heaven' (Matthew 5:16).

In verse 15 Paul says: **Be very careful, then, how you live – not as unwise but as wise.** This takes us back to the very beginning of the chapter when we were told to walk in love. The walk by which we express the Christian life is not that of a carefree, freewheeling attitude, but one that demonstrates sober thinking and careful diligence.

He goes on, **making the most of every opportunity, because the days are evil** (verse 16). This echoes a theme found in the teaching of our Lord himself, particularly in the Sermon on the Mount. Christians are called to live in a context of spiritual crisis. Evil is rampant in the culture around us. As long as the kingdom of God is in conflict with the powers of darkness, it may be said that the days are 'evil'. One of the great emphases of the Sermon on the Mount is that the servant is called to yield the fruits of righteousness and of service in the kingdom of God. We are called to be productive Christian people, and in order to be productive, we must be careful with our use of time. I have as much time in a day as the President of the United States has. To make the most of every opportunity means to make a wise use of time, so that the things we are doing are productive and helpful, not destructive and wasteful.

Therefore do not be foolish, but understand what the Lord's will is. Do not get drunk on wine, which leads to debauchery. Instead, be filled with the Spirit (verses 17, 18). To be drunk with wine is to squander one's life. It is to lose our faculties of consciousness, our clarity of thought and our ability to function. Drunkenness not only causes automobile accidents in which people get maimed and killed, but is also a manifestation of foolishness precisely because we lose control of our thinking and our faculties. Rather we are to be filled with the Holy Spirit, which shows itself when we **Speak to one another with psalms, hymns and spiritual songs** and when we **sing and make music in your heart to the Lord** (verse 19). Isn't it wonderful that the apostle takes time now to enjoin upon us the sheer delight of singing. The learning of hymns and psalms, and the singing of spiritual songs, how enriching that can be to the soul.

Recently I saw a television interview of two young men, both under the age of twenty-one, who are in prison on charges of first-degree murder. One had murdered a sales clerk whom he had never met before, and then gone home and murdered his mother and stepfather. The other murdered his best friend in a brutal act of slaying. Both of these young men revealed that they had become involved in this life of violent crime and first-degree murder as a direct link with their involvement in Satanic, cultic rites and worship. Both of these men had become Christians while they were in prison. But the point is this: they were asked how they moved from their middle-class, suburban, healthy environments to their profound commitment to and involvement in Satanic worship. Both pointed to the same trigger mechanism, the same catalyst, and it was 'heavy metal' music.

It reminded me, as I listened to them, of Plato's concerns

in his own day that people's minds and values were so strongly conditioned by the words and structures of music. Music is a very, very powerful force, and that powerful force can be a force for good or it can be a force for evil. It is not just a matter of indifference or fad. There are different kinds of popular music, and I am not suggesting that all popular music is destructive and harmful and leads to Satanic religion. But extreme forms of anarchist-type themes in music can be extremely destructive to a young person's thinking.

Paul, in contradistinction to that, speaks about the joy of singing among ourselves with psalms and hymns and spiritual songs, making melody to the Lord. We are singing to the Lord, **always giving thanks to God the Father for everything, in the name of our Lord Jesus Christ** (verse 20).

Oftentimes these words are misappropriated to say more than the text actually says. 'For everything' must be interpreted consistent with the last clause, 'in the name of our Lord Jesus Christ'. If the meaning of the term 'for everything' is devoid of reference to God's character, purpose and nature, grave distortions can occur. Some, in 'literal' zeal, actually thank God for things he despises. This faulty thinking drives some to the conclusion they must thank God for the very evil he hates.

May this never be. We dare not thank God for evil consequences of sinful actions, such as when a drunken driver kills another person. What we praise God for is for being God in the midst of such terrible tragedies, and for his redeeming purposes which can bring light out of darkness. There is a multitude of things to thank God for in the midst of tragedies, but these must be consistent with his character and redeeming purposes. Exhaust those things in prayer, and do not be tempted to offer indiscriminate praise to the offence of God.

9
Christian Submission
(5:21–6:9)

Submit to one another out of reverence for Christ.

Wives, submit to your husbands as to the Lord. For the husband is the head of the wife as Christ is the head of the church, his body, of which he is the Saviour. Now as the church submits to Christ, so also wives should submit to their husbands in everything.

Husbands, love your wives, just as Christ loved the church and gave himself up for her to make her holy, cleansing her by the washing with water through the word, and to present her to himself as a radiant church, without stain or wrinkle or any other blemish, but holy and blameless. In this same way, husbands ought to love their wives as their own bodies. He who loves his wife loves himself. After all, no-one ever hated his own body, but he feeds and cares for it, just as Christ does the church — for we are members of his body. "For this reason a man will leave his father and mother and be united to his wife, and the two will become one flesh." This is a profound mystery — but I am talking about Christ and the church. However, each one of you also must love his wife as he loves himself, and the wife must respect her husband.

Children, obey your parents in the Lord, for this is right. "Honour your father and mother" — which is the first commandment with a promise — "that it may go well with you and that you may enjoy long life on the earth."

Fathers, do not exasperate your children; instead, bring them up in the training and instruction of the Lord.

Slaves, obey your earthly masters with respect and fear, and with sincerity of heart, just as you would obey Christ. Obey them not only to win their favour when their eye is on you, but like slaves of Christ, doing the will of God from your heart. Serve wholeheartedly, as if you were serving the Lord, not men, because you know that the Lord will reward everyone for whatever good he does, whether he is slave or free.

And masters, treat your slaves in the same way. Do not threaten them, since you know that he who is both their Master and yours is in heaven, and there is no favouritism with him.

Husbands and wives

In the latter portion of chapter 5 we encounter one of the most controversial passages for today in the whole epistle. It was not very controversial throughout the history of the Christian church, but with the advent of feminism in Western civilisation, it has become extremely controversial. This is because the text, on the surface at least, seems to suggest a hierarchical structure of authority within the home by which, under the law of God, the husband is said to be the head of the house, and the wife is called to be in submission to her husband.

The argument of the feminists is that Paul wrote these instructions not by the inspiration of the Holy Spirit or by the revelation of God but from a standpoint of male arrogance. Chauvinism, whether it be in Paul or other men, assumes that there is an innate or intrinsic superiority of the male gender and a corresponding intrinsic inferiority of the female gender. Therefore the rationale for calling wives to be submissive to their husbands assumes this feminine inferiority.

This objection is based upon two assumptions. The first is that Paul was not setting forth the revelation of God. This assumption is tied to one's view of Sacred Scripture. If one is persuaded that the Bible, including Ephesians, is the Word of God, then one would immediately dismiss this assumption and regard it as slander against the Holy Spirit himself.

The second assumption is that to teach the subordination of the wife to the husband automatically carries the implication of female inferiority. This assumption is manifestly invalid. Though there is no doubt that countless men have chauvinistically drawn this erroneous conclusion from the text, the text itself does not warrant it. Because a person is given a subordinate position in a given structure that involves a division of labour does not carry with it the necessary inference of inferiority. We do not believe that the vice-president of the United States is necessarily inferior, as a human being, to the president of the United States. Children are not inferior to their parents simply because they are under their parents' authority.

The best model we have for this is to be found in the Trinity. In the economy of redemption, the Son is subordinate to the Father, and the Holy Spirit is subordinate to both the Father and the Son. Yet at the same time we insist that the Son and the Spirit are co-eternal, co-essential, and equal in power and dignity with the Father. The Son is not inferior to the Father and the Spirit is not inferior to the Son and the Father.

Another feminist objection is this: Paul was articulating a theology of women derived in part from rabbinic Judaism and in part from the general culture, both of which did regard women as inferior. This is basically a more sophisticated version of the same objection. It is a more subtle way of saying that Paul was a chauvinist who was not writing as an agent of revelation. It mollifies the slander against him slightly by making Paul a victim of the undue influence of rabbinic tradition and the prevailing ideas of his day. Of course, if we carried this assumption to its extreme we would find little or nothing in the New Testament that differs from or transcends the cultural thinking of its day. On the other hand, if we find anything in the writing of Paul it is a thinker who, following Jesus, was so radically innovative and critical of human traditions that it cost him, as it did Jesus before him, his very life.

A more serious objection is that Paul's teaching in Ephesians contradicts his teaching in Galatians. This suggests either that Paul was confused or that his apostolic teaching underwent revisions as he grew in his own understanding of the implications of the gospel. Another alternative is that we, in interpreting Paul, are the ones who are confused and must look to Galatians 3:28 as the controlling principle of interpretation. In Galatians 3:28 we read: 'There is neither Jew nor Greek, slave nor free, male nor female, for you are all one in Christ Jesus.'

Of all the objections raised against Ephesians 5:22, this is the one we hear most frequently. I must confess that the use of the Galatians passage as a rebuttal to Ephesians 5:22 never ceases to amaze me. I see it as the classic illogical conclusion. The reasoning goes something like this: If in Christ there is neither male nor female, this implies that conversion to Christ obliterates the distinction between male and female. Conversion must yield unisexuality or asexuality. Paul, therefore, is caught in a hopeless contradiction between Ephesians and Galatians. On the one hand he teaches that in Christ there is neither male nor female, while on the other hand he enjoins the female member of a marriage (the wife) to be submissive to the male member (the husband).

But the contradiction in poor Paul's thinking doesn't end there. Apparently the confused apostle repeatedly contradicts his teaching of Galatians. Paul frequently gives instructions regarding the relationship between slaves and masters and even wrote an entire letter (Philemon) on the subject. How blatantly inconsistent this would be if Paul believed that distinction to have been obliterated completely. It is true that Paul sowed seeds for the abolition of the institution of slavery. Yet he recognised the fact that there were believers who were still slaves and believers who were still masters. He addressed both on their respective roles.

If we examine the context of Paul's teaching in Galatians we see that he is discussing the cardinal question of salvation by faith in Christ. It should be clear to us that what Paul has in view is this: 'You are all sons of God through faith in Christ Jesus' (Galatians 3:26).

It is by faith in Christ that we are saved. Anyone who has

faith in Christ is included in the family of God. Salvation is not restricted to Jews or to Gentiles, to males or to females, to slaves or to freemen. The great leveller regarding salvation is not race, sexuality or status, but faith. That is the obvious point he is making. To carry his statement that in Christ there is neither male nor female to the absolute degree of the obliteration of the sexes is to do violence to the apostle's own teaching.

I want to look carefully at this text, not with the narrow-minded bigotry of a first century Jew, but as the revelation of the law of God.

Paul says, in verse 21, **Submit to one another out of reverence for Christ**. I have seen modern treatments of this passage that have, in my judgment, entertained a kind of exegesis of Scripture that is utterly irresponsible. Some have linked the whole passage to this phrase, **Submit to one another out of reverence for Christ**, meaning that everything that is enjoined to the wife also applies to the husband. This would mean that wives have to be subject to their husbands and husbands have to be subject to their wives.

No, I think that verse 21 is a general introduction. In order to live the Christian life, each one of us has to manifest subjection to other people at certain points. I have to be in submission to the Presbytery that ordains me, to the Police Department in my town, to the Government of the United States. Everybody at some point has to learn what it means to submit to any authority that is over us in any capacity.

Now how do we flesh that out? Paul says that there is a certain structure which God has ordained, by which wives have to be in submission to their husbands, children to their parents.

This passage should put to rest once and for all the myth that marriages are to be fifty-fifty. I can't think of a worse scenario for a marriage than to have the authority in that relationship divided equally. When two people are together like that, then nobody has any authority. You are in a perpetual power-struggle where one is trying to get control of 51% of the stock. And that can be exceedingly destructive to a family.

When the Bible says that the husband is to be the head of the home, and that the wife is to be in submission to her husband, it does not give the man a licence to tyranny. It does not mean that the man is never to consult with his wife or to lean upon her wisdom and take seriously her concerns and her judgment. When Adam was created, with dominion over the earth, Eve ruled over the earth with him as his helpmate, not as his servant. In a sense, God made Adam king over the creation and gave Eve to him as his queen, not as his slave-girl. There is all the difference in the world between a queen and a slave-girl.

Wives, submit to your husbands as to the Lord (verse 22). This is a service and an act of worship that the woman gives to the Lord himself. It is the Lord's will that the wife be submissive to her husband, and if she wants to honour Christ, then one of the concrete ways she does this is by being in submission to her husband. If a woman is contentious and refuses to follow the leadership of her husband, she is in rebellion, not simply against him, but also against Christ.

Let me make a qualification here. Whenever we are called to obey anyone, be it a civil magistrate, a domestic leader or our church rulers, we are told in the whole context of Scripture that we must ultimately be submissive to God. So if there is ever a conflict between the law of God and the rule of a human being, not only may you disobey, you must disobey the human command.

There is a teaching which has gone widely through evangelical Christianity which says that for a woman to be obedient to this passage, she must obey her husband no matter what he tells her to do. This is not true. For example, if her husband tells her to live a life of prostitution, she is to show her obedience to Christ by disobeying her husband's wicked commands. That woman must disobey her husband, because her husband is commanding her to do something that God forbids. Similarly, if the husband forbids her to do something that God commands, she must disobey her husband.

Nevertheless, the general principle is that a woman is to bend over backwards to defer to the leadership and authority of her husband. She is not free to disobey simply because she disagrees or because she finds herself inconvenienced by what the husband requires.

Why? The reason Paul gives is this: **For the husband is the head of the wife as Christ is the head of the church, his body, of which he is the Saviour. Now as the church submits to Christ, so also wives should submit to their husbands in everything** (verses 23, 24). There is an analogy between the headship of Christ over the church and the headship of the husband over the wife. All kinds of exegetical gymnastics have been attempted in order to try to vitiate this passage, but here it is: headship involves authority. This authority is not given to exercise tyranny, but leadership. The husband is responsible for the leadership of the home. He is accountable to God for how the home is managed, and how the affairs of the home are conducted.

Here's where the men want to stop reading: **Husbands, love your wives, just as Christ loved the church and gave himself up for her** (verse 25). No Christian woman would object for a single moment to be in submission to her husband, if her husband were Jesus Christ. Obviously the Bible calls wives to be in subjection to husbands who are not Jesus Christ, but the responsibility that is given to the man here is terrifying: to love their wives like Christ loved the church and gave himself for the church. Would a woman be afraid to submit herself to a man who loved her as much as Jesus loved the church? Would a woman fight and kick and scream against the leadership of a man who was willing to give his lifeblood to do anything he could to save her life? The kind of rule that the husband is to have over his wife is to be modelled on the leadership of Jesus.

Some husbands respond, 'I'll love my wife as Christ loved the church, as soon as she starts to submit herself to me!' But that's not how Christ loved the church. Christ loved a church that was not submissive to him. Christ died for a church that was in rebellion against him. Some wives will say, 'I will subject myself to my husband, when he starts loving me.' No, they have a responsibility before God to conduct themselves according to the word of God in their marriage.

Why did Christ die? **To make her holy, cleansing her by the washing with water through the word, and to present her to himself as a radiant church, without stain or wrinkle or any other blemish, but holy and blameless** (verses 26, 27).

Ceremonial baths were a regular feature in Jewish customs. Probably Paul is alluding here to the particular bath a bride underwent prior to her marriage ceremony. Symbolically, defilement was washed away, and purity was reinstated.

For the Christian, Paul may be saying that a similar cleansing unto holiness is effected by two agencies: the 'washing of water' and 'through the word'. Baptism, the washing of water, is said by Calvin to be the outward symbol by which the inner and invisible work of sanctification is confirmed. This external rite must, however, be accompanied by the second means, the application of the word of the gospel. Scripture becomes the means by which the Spirit accomplishes his work of sanctification–the process of becoming holy and blameless. Diligent attention to the Scriptures is the ordained means by which God conforms us to the image of his Son, burning away the dross of sin that so thoroughly pollutes our lives. Jesus' intention for his bride is to present her to the Father in her full splendour, without spot or wrinkle. He only wants the best for her.

That is the pattern that husbands are to follow: **In this same way, husbands ought to love their wives as their own bodies. He who loves his wife loves himself. After all, no-one ever hated his own body, but he feeds and cares for it, just as Christ does the church** (verses 28, 29). One of the most wonderful parts of the marriage ceremony is the vow that we take to cherish one another. To cherish one another means to hold one another in the highest esteem and to place an infinite value on one another. This is the attitude that is to permeate the home. Not a power struggle or a see-saw battle for more authority than the other one. Rather, the man is to love his wife as he loves his own flesh. A man takes care of his own flesh. He feeds himself, eats, drinks, nourishes his body and protects it. He has a strong instinct of self-preservation. He is to love his wife even more than he loves himself.

'For this reason a man will leave his father and mother and be united to his wife, and the two will become one flesh.' The mystical goal of marriage is the union of two people. That union does not annul or annihilate individual personalities. This stands in stark contrast to Eastern religions where the loss of personal identity takes place in the mystical union of marriage. In Christianity, the union is very profound. People become of one mind, one concern, and one passion. That goes deep in a healthy marriage; the two are like one person.

This is a profound mystery – but I am talking about Christ and the church (verse 32). Notice how Paul keeps weaving this theme through Ephesians. Earlier he had talked about the church as the body of Christ in the mystical union that is shared by all who participate in fellowship with Christ (see pages 88–91).

However, each one of you also must love his wife as he loves himself, and the wife must respect her husband (verse 33). Probably the most fragile mechanism in the whole creation is the male ego. One of the most difficult things to admit or to understand is that there is probably nothing that a man wants more from his wife than her admiration. There is probably nothing that a woman wants more from her husband than his attention, taking her seriously and treating her with the greatest dignity. Here what we are getting at is the question of respect. If I exercise my headship over my wife in a tyrannical way, I am not respecting my wife. If my wife gives slavish obedience to me without any love, she is not respecting me. The whole basis of the relationship is built upon love, cherishing and respecting one another.

Parents and children

Children, obey your parents in the Lord, for this is right. 'Honour your father and mother' – which is the first commandment with a promise – 'that it may go well with you and that you may enjoy long life on the earth' (6:1-3). The rendering of obedience to one's parents is not simply a social convention, but it is a duty that is to be rendered to God. So important did God deem this particular duty of mankind, that he included it in the ten commandments, the foundation of the law for his nation, Israel. The respect that children are to give to their parents is essential for a well-ordered society, for the stability of the home, and also for the development of discipline and character in children. Notice the way the apostle says this: 'Children, obey your parents in the Lord, for this is right'. It is proper, it is good, for children to render obedience to their parents. He cites the fifth commandment:

'Honour your father and mother' – which is the first commandment with a promise – 'that it may go well with you and that you may enjoy long life on the earth.'

But Paul doesn't stop with the responsibilities of children to their parents. He goes on: **Fathers, do not exasperate your children; instead, bring them up in the training and instruction of the Lord** (verse 4).

The father is held accountable by God as the one who is responsible for teaching the children and for being the disciplinarian of the children. Fathers are warned at this point that as they carry out these responsibilities of discipline and instruction, they are not to be tyrannical or harsh in their treatment of the children.

We read countless passages in the Old Testament that warn against a latitudinarian spirit by which parents are so permissive that they refuse to discipline unruly children. Remember the statement that the parent who will not discipline his child, hates the child (Proverbs 13:24). Parents, when they are disciplining their children, often say, 'This hurts me more than it hurts you.' That really is true. There are times when parents find it extremely difficult to discipline their children because they don't want to alienate the children and they don't want to put up with the tears that may follow from disciplinary action. But when they just allow children to do whatever they want, without any discipline and without any instruction, they are loving themselves rather than their children.

So we have a host of admonitions in Scripture that call parents to be very diligent in the administration of discipline to their children. But with this caveat, **do not exasperate your children**. This doesn't mean that every time a child becomes angry with a parent, it is because the parents have been guilty of unjust provocation. But there is such a thing as a belligerent, insensitive, harsh, and stentorian type of discipline which so frustrates children that they are filled with hostility and resentment towards their parents which then spills over into the rest of their lives. Of course, the ultimate model of discipline and chastisement is God himself, who always tempers his wrath with mercy.

Masters and servants

Some people find verses 5-6 very, very difficult to deal with at all, because we have this admonition: **Slaves, obey your earthly masters with respect and fear, and with sincerity of heart, just as you would obey Christ. Obey them not only to win their favour when their eye is on you, but like slaves of Christ, doing the will of God from your heart.** At the time this was written, slavery was a commonplace social phenomenon. This tends to rub against the grain for contemporary Christians who see the very institution of slavery as something utterly inconsistent with the gospel and the will of God. Yet it seems by implication here that Paul is endorsing some forms of the institution of slavery.

There were certain kinds of voluntary slavery in the ancient world, where a person would bind himself over to the service of another person, for example, to pay off his debts. But there was also the whole idea of selling people into slavery and the even worse practice of stealing people who were free and using them as slaves. Paul doesn't comment here on any of the variety of forms of slavery that did exist in the ancient world. He just speaks in general to anyone who happens to be in that situation of slavery.

John Murray deals with this subject in his book *Principles of Conduct*. Murray says that Paul doesn't speak for or against slavery here in this passage, he is simply addressing those who happen to be in that particular situation. If you are a slave, whether justly or unjustly, you are still under the authority of your designated master, and as such it is your duty to perform the services that are expected and required of you. That is the Christian way for slaves to behave. Murray goes on to say that, in spite of Paul's instructions here to slaves and in spite of his writing an entire letter (Philemon) concerning a runaway slave, the New Testament in general, and Paul's writings in particular, contained the seeds of the dissolution of the institution of slavery. Subsequent history demonstrates that the Christian church has been at the forefront of the movement for the abolition of this institution.

Paul is speaking consistently about rendering service to whom service is due. Now we can speak more broadly here. There is a sense in which anyone who is in the employ of another person, although not a slave, is in a situation where services are to be rendered. In the case of our twentieth century industrial contracts, those services are rendered for hire. Employees receive pay cheques from their employers who enter into an agreement with those whom they employ. Employees are committed to giving certain services in return for the benefits and the remuneration that they receive for those services. Some of the principles that Paul applies to slaves can well be carried over and applied to anyone who is an employee. What Paul says is this: Work with sincerity of heart, just as you would obey Christ. Wherever Christians are rendering a service, they must understand that such service is ultimately presented, not to employers or owners, but to Christ. So that by serving our masters or employers well, we are thereby rendering a service to Christ.

In verse 6, Paul writes: **Obey them not only to win their favour when their eye is on you, but like slaves of Christ, doing the will of God from your heart**. All of us tend to perform more diligently when the eyes of our supervisors are upon us. But when there is no-one there to give oversight, we may slack off and shirk our responsibilities. Often, the only thing that keeps employees diligent and responsible in their work is the fact that somebody is watching them. But Paul is saying, 'Look, a real servant is somebody who works to please God. If you are going to please God it doesn't matter whether a supervisor is present or not present, for God is always looking at the heart.' We are expected, as Christians, to be people of integrity, doing a full day's work, whether somebody is watching over our shoulders or not **because you know that the Lord will reward everyone for whatever good he does, whether he is slave or free** (verse 8).

Paul also has a word for those who are masters of slaves, and if we want to apply it more broadly, that would be to employers: **And masters, treat your slaves in the same way. Do not threaten them, since you know that he who is both their Master and yours is in heaven, and there is no favouritism with him** (verse 9). Whether a master has 50 slaves, or an employer 5,000 employees, both are still under the authority of the supreme Master. The employer is commanded to treat those who are under his authority in the same manner that he hopes to be treated by his Master in heaven. When I was working closely with Wayne Alderson and the Value of the Person movement in labour and management in Western Pennsylvania, I used to think frequently about this question: How would a steel mill function in terms of lines of authority and treatment of subordinates if Christ were the superintendent of that particular factory?

Sometimes we think that if Jesus were the boss of a work project, he would be so kind, gentle, and gracious that he wouldn't expect any work. But just a cursory glance at the New Testament, where Jesus is constantly urging his people to be productive and diligent in their labour, would show Jesus to be a demanding superintendent. He would expect those who were under his authority to give honest effort and a full day's work. Yet at the same time, there would be no partiality, no injustice, no petty criticisms, and no demeaning attacks on people's dignity. He is the perfect Master who treats all those under his authority with love, tenderness, gentleness, justice and righteousness. He is the model for anyone who is in a position of authority.

10
Christian Warfare
(6:10-24)

Finally, be strong in the Lord and in his mighty power. Put on the full armour of God so that you can take your stand against the devil's schemes. For our struggle is not against flesh and blood, but against the rulers, against the authorities, against the powers of this dark world and against the spiritual forces of evil in the heavenly realms. Therefore put on the full armour of God, so that when the day of evil comes, you may be able to stand your ground, and after you have done everything, to stand. Stand firm then, with the belt of truth buckled round your waist, with the breastplate of righteousness in place, and with your feet fitted with the readiness that comes from the gospel of peace. In addition to all this, take up the shield of faith, with which you can extinguish all the flaming arrows of the evil one. Take the helmet of salvation and the sword of the Spirit, which is the word of God. And pray in the Spirit on all occasions with all kinds of prayers and requests. With this in mind, be alert and always keep on praying for all the saints.

Pray also for me, that whenever I open my mouth, words may be given me so that I will fearlessly make known the mystery of the gospel, for which I am an ambassador in chains. Pray that I may declare it fearlessly, as I should.

Tychicus, the dear brother and faithful servant in the Lord, will tell you everything, so that you also may know how I am and what I am doing. I am sending him to you for this very purpose, that you may know how we are, and that he may encourage you.

Peace to the brothers, and love with faith from God the Father and the Lord Jesus Christ. Grace to all who love our Lord Jesus Christ with an undying love.

Paul is now concluding his letter. He urges his readers: **Finally, be strong in the Lord and in his mighty power.** The strength we are to manifest as Christians is the strength that is found in and through Christ. Why Christians need strength is explained here in one of the most magnificent treatments in the entire Bible of the Christian life in terms of warfare. Paul takes common elements of battle garb from the Roman soldier and gives a spiritual application to each one.

He begins: **Put on the full armour of God.** The term for 'full armour' in the Greek is the word from which we get the English word 'panoply', the complete battle-gear of the warrior. Paul is obviously using an analogy drawn from his own experience of Roman soldiers. Sometimes we think of armour as what a medieval knight would wear to protect himself against attack. But the panoply of a Roman soldier included both his defensive gear and his offensive weaponry. To be involved in this cosmic struggle where we are wrestling against powers and principalities, against demonic forces, we must be fully prepared and fully dressed for the battle.

The reason, he says, is this: **so that you can take your stand against the devil's schemes. For our struggle is not against flesh and blood, but against the rulers, against the authorities, against the powers of this dark world and against the spiritual forces of evil in the heavenly realms** (verses 11, 12). He is talking about cosmic warfare. Each Christian is a target of Satan and his angels, and this struggle goes on throughout one's lifetime. If we are to stand firm we have to be properly equipped for that battle. **Therefore,** he repeats, **put on the full armour of God, so that when the day of evil comes, you may be able to stand your ground, and after you have done everything, to stand** (verse 13).

Paul begins with **stand firm then, with the belt of truth**

buckled round your waist (verse 14). The standard form of dress in the ancient world for the Jews as well as for the Romans, was a robe. Imagine a soldier trying to move quickly and deftly in battle, while his legs are getting caught in this flowing robe. When it was time to go into battle, the soldiers pulled their robes above their knees, and gathered the folds of the robe tightly around their waists with a heavy belt. Paul is saying that the first thing believers need to do is to get ready to move into battle. That which makes it possible to move, is truth.

Now what truth does Paul have in mind here? Commentators vary in this. Some say it is the truth of theology or a true understanding of the things of God in the gospel that gives the ability to be agile in the field of attack, to be able to move quickly when Satan is throwing his darts. Others say it could refer to truth in the sense of *living the truth*. In other words, personal integrity. The person who is involved in spiritual warfare, but is weighted down with his own sinfulness, is like someone trying to run through a battlefield with a robe around his ankles.

Whether it refers to theological truth, spiritual truth or the truth of personal character, the point Paul stresses is that the truth is the first piece of armour with which we need to gird ourselves.

With the breastplate of righteousness in place (verse 14). The breastplate in a Roman soldier's armour was the heavy section that fitted over his torso. Its chief purpose was to protect the vital organs of the body from being pierced by an arrow or a sword or other weapons. Paul says that Christians need to protect their vital areas with righteousness. Remember the classic story of the great hero, Achilles, who seemed to be invincible. The legend is that his mother, when he was a baby, dipped him into some kind of magical potion that coated his entire body with an invincible shield. But when she dipped him into this substance, she held him by the tip of his heel, so that one portion of his body was not covered with the magic solution. It was there that, in the course of a great battle in the Trojan War, Achilles was struck in the heel by an arrow and was slain. He had one uncovered point on his body where he was vulnerable. When believers are living in unconfessed sin, they are vulnerable to the assaults of Satan.

And with your feet fitted with the readiness that comes from the gospel of peace (verse 15). Today, war is carried on for the most part in a highly mechanised manner. Up until the modern era, however, perhaps the single most important dimension of warfare was the march. For example, Stonewall Jackson distinguished himself in the annals of American warfare by his incredible prowess in moving troops quickly and strategically from one site to another. In the ancient world, armies had elephants (as Hannibal had, for example), ships and other forms of mobilisation. But for the most part, the effective army in the ancient world moved by foot. Soldiers were indeed called 'foot soldiers'. So, if the protection of the feet was inadequate, then the army was not able to carry out its mission.

I remember, during the Korean conflict in 1950-51, seeing vivid photographs of severe cases of frostbite which were incurred by American foot soldiers in Korea. One of the problems that the American combat soldier experienced in the Korean conflict was due to the climate of those particular zones. The areas were so damp that when the temperature lowered, wet shoes froze. Next, the feet froze. Hence, the problem that the soldiers had to deal with in the battle was not the guns of the enemy but their own inadequate clothing.

What Paul says we are to use for the covering of our feet if we are going to remain mobile and adroit in our activity, is the gospel of peace. This has its roots in ancient imagery. In Romans 10:15, Paul quotes from Isaiah 52:7 about the necessity of the office of preaching: 'And how can they preach unless they are sent? As it is written, "How beautiful are the feet of those who bring good news!" ' That image drawn from the Old Testament can be traced back to the communications system of the ancient world, particularly with respect to battle line communications. When armies went to battle, those who remained at home waited anxiously to hear of the outcome, because often their destiny was tied to the success or failure of the armies. But they didn't have telecommunication systems that could rush news instantly from the battlefront back to the local community. So messages were carried by runners.

In the ancient world it was customary, in some places, that if the messenger brought bad news, he was punished with death. If it was bad news, then, he would be burdened by the news that he was carrying, and fearful of what treatment he might expect. As each city posted lookouts to watch the approaching runners, it became almost a science whereby the lookout could determine whether the messenger was bringing good news or bad news, just by his feet. If the messenger was bringing good news of victory, his feet would be flying and he would be kicking up a lot of dust. There would be an exuberance and an enthusiasm in his gait, as he approached the walls of the city. Hence the phrase, 'How beautiful are the feet of those who bring good news!'

Paul is saying that there is nothing more beautiful to see than a messenger who is bringing good news, and that is what the word 'gospel' means. It is the good news of the peace that we have with God, having been reconciled to the Father by the work of Jesus. The gospel becomes that which protects our feet, covers our feet and makes us mobile in the battle against cosmic evil.

In addition to all this, take up the shield of faith (verse 16). The shield was a defensive part of the equipment of the soldier. One feature of the Roman armies was the phalanx, a close quarter arrangement in which the soldiers would march against a city. Their shields were not little round shields that gladiators used in the arena or medieval knights used for jousting, but they were rectangular shields, about six or eight feet high, three to four feet wide. They were not simply held out in front of the soldiers as they marched, but rather, as they approached a city, the soldiers would hold their shields side-by-side to stop spears, rocks and arrows that were being shot at them from the citadel. Then, as they approached the walls of the city, they would raise the shields over their heads, because of objects that would be thrown down on them.

The shield that protects believers from Satan's attacks is the shield of faith **with which you can extinguish all the flaming arrows of the evil one** (verse 16). In battle, torch arrows were fired into the enemy's ranks to set the clothes of the soldiers on fire. They were also fired into the city where they could wreak havoc and panic among the inhabitants. The analogy here is that Satan doesn't just throw darts that can wound and penetrate, but flaming darts that can burn and sear and scar us deeply. The way we overcome all of these things that assail us, as we seek to live out the Christian life, is by the shield of faith. What protects us from the enemy is our trust in the living God.

One of the most formidable weapons of Satan is the weapon of accusation. In the book of Zechariah, Joshua the high priest was accused by Satan, who went to God and said, 'Look at your high priest, he is wearing filthy garments, he is not fit for your service and for your kingdom' (Zechariah 3:1-5). Satan accuses believers of their sin and their unworthiness to belong to the kingdom of God. He does this, not to lead them to repentance but to lead them to despair, so that they will be paralysed and not able to function effectively as Christians. The only answer we have to these attacks of Satan against our integrity is that we are justified by faith. Our saving faith in Christ is the shield that protects us from the accusations of the enemy.

Take the helmet of salvation (verse 17). The helmet protected the head, where it was so easy to deliver a fatal blow. Although Satan cannot kill the soul, he can wound the mind. Those who are in a state of salvation have their minds covered by the salvation (past, present and future) that has been wrought for them in Christ.

Paul then moves to the offensive weapon of the soldier, the sword. A sword was used, not simply as a defensive precaution, but to cut through the defences of the enemy. Paul speaks of **the sword of the Spirit, which is the word of God** (verse 17). Jesus himself, when he was beset by Satan, foiled him with the word of God. He used Scripture to disarm Satan who could not stand against the counter force of Scripture.

Together with all of these pieces of equipment that make up the full armour of God, we are to **pray in the Spirit on all occasions with all kinds of prayers and requests** (verse 18). All of our warfare and all of our activity must take place in the context of constant, unceasing prayer. Just as a soldier on the battle line has to keep in constant communication with his general headquarters and his commanding officer, so the Christian who is on the battle line must be in constant communication with his Lord. He might be fully equipped with all of the armour, but if he is cut off from personal communication with his own commander, then he will be isolated and vulnerable.

To *pray in the Spirit* does not mean praying in tongues. Praying in the Spirit means that the Spirit helps us to communicate with the Father, interceding for us. When Paul tells us to pray in the Spirit it reminds us of what Jesus said to the woman at the well, that we are called to worship God in Spirit and in truth. Not in a perfunctory manner, not by reciting our favourite syllables or empty repetitions, but praying from the depths of our souls. To pray in concert with the Holy Spirit means that the communication is earnest in its origin and in its passion.

Prayer is not a meaningless exercise. We are to **be alert and always keep on praying for all the saints** (verse 18). We are not just to be praying for ourselves, but for all of those who are part of the fellowship of the household of God.

Then Paul makes a personal request in verse 19: **Pray also for me, that whenever I open my mouth, words may be given me so that I will fearlessly make known the mystery of the gospel**. If ever there was a request answered by the people of God, it was this call to prayer. Who has ever preached the gospel with greater perseverance and with greater boldness than the apostle Paul? Even while he was in chains in prison, Paul was preaching the gospel.

Verse 20 says, **for which I am an ambassador in chains**. What an image! When people go to Washington, the capital of the United States, and look at the ornate buildings that decorate what is called Embassy Row, and see the uniforms that the diplomats wear on the various formal occasions, they fall over themselves to make a visiting ambassador feel like a dignitary. We accord great respect to their office. The greatest ambassador in history, apart from Jesus himself, is Paul who now goes into the highest political centre in the world at that time, into Rome itself. And he comes into that city, not with formal dress or with the uniform of a visiting dignitary, but in chains. He asks his friends to pray for him that, even when he is in chains, he will deliver the message that the King has commissioned him to speak. **Pray that I may declare it fearlessly, as I should**. There is a moral imperative to be bold with the proclamation of the gospel, rather than mealy-mouthed or apologetic.

Tychicus, the dear brother and faithful servant in the

Lord (verse 21) was one of Paul's closest associates. He speaks of him on other occasions (Colossians 4:7; 2 Timothy 4:12; Titus 3:12) and obviously he was known to the readers. To get a visit from Tychicus was the next best thing to getting a visit from Paul himself. Paul is saying, 'Now, look, this is the end of the letter. If you want to know more about how I am doing personally and how I am holding up under my imprisonment and how things look for the future, Tychicus will fill you in on all of the details.' He **will tell you everything, so that you also may know how I am and what I am doing. I am sending him to you for this very purpose, that you may know how we are, and that he may encourage you** (verses 21, 22).

Then, in verses 23 and 24, Paul concludes the letter with his customary benediction: **Peace to the brothers, and love with faith from God the Father and the Lord Jesus Christ.** Paul closes his epistle with the combination of perhaps his two favourite words (words which have their roots in the Old Testament): grace and peace. It was the great desire of every Jew to understand, to know, and to experience a lasting peace; not only a cessation of warfare with foreign enemies, but a cessation of warfare with God himself. Paul says, 'This is my prayer for you that you will be nurtured and grow and that you will know the peace of God.' But he adds to this customary closing, the conjoining of love and faith.

A benediction is not a prayer. A benediction means 'a good saying' and is a prophetic utterance. When the apostle gives his apostolic benediction to his readers or to his hearers he is speaking as an ambassador of the King. He is announcing God's benediction upon his people. So when Paul refers to peace and grace and love and faith, he is not saying, 'Grace to you and peace from *me*.' But he is announcing that the promise of grace, peace, faith, and love comes from God the Father and the Lord Jesus Christ. He is, therefore, speaking for both the Father and the Son.

Grace to all who love our Lord Jesus Christ with an undying love, that is, with a love that is real. The love of Christ that is shed abroad in our hearts by the Holy Spirit is not a passing fad or a romantic infatuation, but it is an enduring and abiding love that perseveres.

Thematic Index

Books
by
R. C. Sproul
published
by
Christian Focus

A Walk With Jesus

376 pages   ISBN 1 85792 260 3   large hardback

A study of the life of Christ, based on the
Gospel of Luke, divided into 104 sections.

Mighty Christ

144 pages   ISBN 1 85792 148 8   paperback

A study of the person and work of Jesus.

The Mystery of the Holy Spirit

192 pages   ISBN 1 871676 63 0   paperback

Examines the role of the Spirit in creation,
salvation and in strengthening the believer..

The Gospel of God

256 pages   ISBN 1 85792 077 5   large hardback

An exposition of the Book of Romans

.